教育部、国家语委重大文化工程
　　"中华思想文化术语传播工程"成果
国家社会科学基金重大项目
　　"中国核心术语国际影响力研究"（21&ZD158）
"十四五"国家重点出版物出版规划项目
获评第二届向全国推荐中华优秀传统文化普及图书

典藏版 · 第一卷

Key Concepts in Chinese Thought and Culture

中华思想文化术语 4

《中华思想文化术语》编委会 编

外语教学与研究出版社
FOREIGN LANGUAGE TEACHING AND RESEARCH PRESS
北京 BEIJING

图书在版编目（CIP）数据

中华思想文化术语：典藏版. 第一卷. 4：汉英对照 /《中华思想文化术语》编委会编. -- 北京：外语教学与研究出版社，2023.12
 ISBN 978-7-5213-4878-1

I. ①中… II. ①中… III. ①中华文化－术语－汉、英 IV. ①K203-61

中国国家版本馆 CIP 数据核字 (2023) 第 205211 号

出 版 人	王　芳
项目策划	刘旭璐
责任编辑	赵璞玉
责任校对	王海燕
封面设计	梧桐影
版式设计	孙莉明
出版发行	外语教学与研究出版社
社　　址	北京市西三环北路 19 号（100089）
网　　址	https://www.fltrp.com
印　　刷	三河市北燕印装有限公司
开　　本	710×1000　1/16
印　　张	57
版　　次	2024 年 1 月第 1 版　2024 年 1 月第 1 次印刷
书　　号	ISBN 978-7-5213-4878-1
定　　价	349.00 元（全五册）

如有图书采购需求，图书内容或印刷装订等问题，侵权、盗版书籍等线索，请拨打以下电话或关注官方服务号：
客服电话：400 898 7008
官方服务号：微信搜索并关注公众号"外研社官方服务号"
外研社购书网址：https://fltrp.tmall.com

物料号：348780001

"中华思想文化术语传播工程"专家团队
(按音序)

Scholars Participating in the Project "Key Concepts in Chinese Thought and Culture: Communication Through Translation"

顾问 (Advisors)

李学勤 (Li Xueqin)　　　　　林戊荪 (Lin Wusun)
叶嘉莹 (Florence Chia-ying Yeh)　张岂之 (Zhang Qizhi)
楼宇烈 (Lou Yulie)　　　　　王　宁 (Wang Ning)

专家委员会 (Committee of Scholars)

主任 (Director)

韩　震 (Han Zhen)

委员 (Members)

晁福林 (Chao Fulin)　　　陈德彰 (Chen Dezhang)
陈明明 (Chen Mingming)　冯志伟 (Feng Zhiwei)
韩经太 (Han Jingtai)　　 黄友义 (Huang Youyi)
金元浦 (Jin Yuanpu)　　　静　炜 (Jing Wei)
李建中 (Li Jianzhong)　　李雪涛 (Li Xuetao)
李照国 (Li Zhaoguo)　　　聂长顺 (Nie Changshun)
潘公凯 (Pan Gongkai)　　 王　博 (Wang Bo)

王柯平（Wang Keping）　　　叶　朗（Ye Lang）
袁济喜（Yuan Jixi）　　　　袁行霈（Yuan Xingpei）
张　晶（Zhang Jing）　　　 张立文（Zhang Liwen）
张西平（Zhang Xiping）　　 郑述谱（Zheng Shupu）

特邀汉学家（Scholars of China Studies）

艾　恺（Guy Salvatore Alitto）　　安乐哲（Roger T. Ames）
白罗米（Luminița Bălan）　　　　包华石（Martin Joseph Powers）
陈瑞河（Madaras Réka）　　　　　狄伯杰（B. R. Deepak）
顾　彬（Wolfgang Kubin）　　　　韩安德（Harry Anders Hansson）
韩　裴（Petko Todorov Hinov）　 柯鸿冈（Paul Crook）
柯马凯（Michael Crook）　　　　 斯巴修（Iljaz Spahiu）
王健、李盈（Jan & Yvonne Walls）　魏查理（Charles Willemen）

学术委员会（Academic Committee）

白振奎（Bai Zhenkui）　　　蔡力坚（Cai Lijian）
曹轩梓（Cao Xuanzi）　　　 陈海燕（Chen Haiyan）
陈少明（Chen Shaoming）　　程景牧（Cheng Jingmu）
丁　浩（Ding Hao）　　　　 付志斌（Fu Zhibin）
干春松（Gan Chunsong）　　 郭晓东（Guo Xiaodong）
韩志华（Han Zhihua）　　　 何　淼（He Miao）
何世剑（He Shijian）　　　 胡　海（Hu Hai）
贾德忠（Jia Dezhong）　　　姜海龙（Jiang Hailong）
柯修文（Daniel Canaris）　 黎　臻（Li Zhen）

李存山（Li Cunshan）	李恭忠（Li Gongzhong）
李景林（Li Jinglin）	林敏洁（Lin Minjie）
林少阳（Lin Shaoyang）	刘　佳（Liu Jia）
刘　璐（Liu Lu）	刘　青（Liu Qing）
吕玉华（Lü Yuhua）	梅缵月（Mei Zuanyue）
孟庆楠（Meng Qingnan）	裴德思（Thorsten Pattberg）
彭冬林（Peng Donglin）	乔　希（Joshua Mason）
任大援（Ren Dayuan）	邵亦鹏（Shao Yipeng）
沈卫星（Shen Weixing）	施晓菁（Lynette Shi）
陶黎庆（Tao Liqing）	童孝华（Tong Xiaohua）
王丽丽（Wang Lili）	王　琳（Wang Lin）
王明杰（Wang Mingjie）	王维东（Wang Weidong）
王　鑫（Wang Xin）	温海明（Wen Haiming）
吴根友（Wu Genyou）	吴礼敬（Wu Lijing）
夏　晶（Xia Jing）	谢远笋（Xie Yuansun）
辛红娟（Xin Hongjuan）	徐明强（Xu Mingqiang）
徐亚男（Xu Yanan）	许家星（Xu Jiaxing）
严学军（Yan Xuejun）	张　静（Zhang Jing）
张子尧（Zhang Ziyao）	章思英（Zhang Siying）
章伟文（Zhang Weiwen）	赵　桐（Zhao Tong）
赵　悠（Zhao You）	郑　开（Zheng Kai）
周云帆（Zhou Yunfan）	朱绩崧（Zhu Jisong）
朱良志（Zhu Liangzhi）	朱　渊（Zhu Yuan）
左　励（Zuo Li）	

前言

"中华思想文化术语"的定义可以表述为：由中华民族所创造或构建，凝聚、浓缩了中华哲学思想、人文精神、思维方式、价值观念，以词或短语形式固化的概念和文化核心词。它们是中华民族几千年来对自然与社会进行探索和理性思索的成果，积淀着中华民族的历史智慧，反映中华民族最深沉的精神追求以及理性思索的深度与广度；其所蕴含的人文思想、思维方式、价值观念已经作为一种"生命基因"深深融于中华子孙的血液，内化为中华民族共同的性格和信仰，并由此支撑起中华数千年的学术传统、思想文化和精神世界。它是当代中国人理解中国古代哲学思想、人文精神、思维方式、价值观念之变化乃至文学艺术、历史等各领域发展的核心关键，也是世界其他国家和民族了解当代中国、中华民族和海外华人之精神世界的钥匙。

当今世界已进入文化多元与话语多极时代。世界不同区域、不同国家、不同民族的文明，其流动融合之快、之广、之深超过历史任何时期。每个国家和民族都有自己独具的思想文化和话语体系，都应在世界文明、世界话语体系中占有一席之地，得到它应有的地位和尊重。而思想文化术语无疑是一个国家和民族话语体系中最核心、最本质的部分，是它的思想之"髓"、文化之"根"、精神之"魂"、学术之"核"。越来越多的有识之士认识到，中华思想文化蕴藏着解决当今人类所面临的许多难题的重要启示，中华民族所倡导的"厚德载物""道法自然""天人合一""和而不同""民惟邦本""经世致用"等思想，以及它所追求的"协和万邦""天下一家"、世界"大同"，代表了当今世界文明的发展趋势，也因此成为国际社会的共识。越来越多的外国学者和友人对中华思想文化及其术语产生浓厚的兴趣，希望有更全面、更进一步的了解。

今天我们整理、诠释、翻译、传播中华思想文化术语，目的是立足于中华思想文化，通过全面系统的整理与诠释，深度挖掘其中既能反映中华哲学思想、人文精神、思维方式、价值观念、文化特征，又具跨越时空、超越国度之意义，以及富有永恒魅力与当代价值的含义和内容，并将其译成英语等语言，让世界更客观、更全面地认识中国，了解中华民族的过去和现在，了解当代中国人及海外华人的精神世界，从而推动国家间的平等对话及不同文明间的交流借鉴。

中华思想文化术语的整理、诠释和英语翻译得到了中国教育部、中国国际出版集团、中央编译局、北京大学、中国人民大学、武汉大学、北京外国语大学等单位的大力支持，得到了叶嘉莹、李学勤、张岂之、林戊荪、楼宇烈、王宁等海内外众多知名学者的支持。需要说明的是，"中华思想文化术语"这个概念是首次提出，其内涵和外延还有待学界更深入的研究；而且，如此大规模地整理、诠释、翻译中华思想文化术语，在中国也是首次，无成例可循。因此，我们的诠释与翻译一定还有待完善的地方，我们会及时吸纳广大读者的意见，不断提高术语诠释与翻译的质量。

2021年12月11日

Foreword

By "key concepts in Chinese thought and culture" we mean concepts and keywords or phrases the Chinese people have created or come to use and that are fundamentally pertinent to Chinese philosophy, humanistic spirit, way of thinking, and values. They represent the Chinese people's exploration of and rational thinking about nature and society over thousands of years. These concepts and expressions reflect the Chinese people's wisdom, their profound spiritual pursuit, as well as the depth and width of their thinking. Their way of thinking, values, and philosophy embodied in these concepts have become a kind of "life gene" in Chinese culture, and have long crystallized into the common personality and beliefs of the Chinese nation. For the Chinese people today, they serve as a key to a better understanding of the evolutions of their ancient philosophy, humanistic spirit, way of thinking, and values as well as the development of Chinese literature, art, and history. For people in other countries, these concepts open the door to understanding the spiritual world of contemporary China and the Chinese people, including those living overseas.

In the era of cultural diversity and multipolar discourse today, cultures of different countries and civilizations of different peoples are integrating faster, in greater depth, and on a greater scope than ever before. All countries and peoples have their own systems of thought, culture, and discourse, which should all have their place in the civilization and discourse systems of the world. They all deserve due respect. The concepts in thought and culture of a country and its people are naturally the most essential part of their discourse. They constitute the marrow of a nation's thought, the root of its culture, the soul of its spirit, and the core of its scholarship. More and more people of vision have come to recognize the inspirations Chinese thought and culture might offer to help resolve many difficult problems faced by mankind. The Chinese hold that a man should "have ample virtue and carry all things," "Dao operates naturally," "heaven and man are united as one," a man of virtue seeks "harmony but not uniformity," "people are the foundation of the state," and "study of ancient classics should meet present needs." The Chinese ideals such as "coexistence of all in harmony," "all the people under heaven are one family," and a world of "universal harmony" are drawing increasing attention among the international community. More and more international scholars and friends have become interested in learning and better understanding Chinese thought and culture in general, and the relevant concepts in particular.

In selecting, explaining, translating, and sharing concepts in Chinese thought and culture, we have adopted a comprehensive and systematic approach. Most of them not only reflect the characteristics of Chinese philosophy, humanistic spirit, way of thinking, values, and culture, but also have significance and/or implications that transcend time and national boundaries, and that still fascinate present-day readers and offer them food for thought. It is hoped that the translation of these concepts into English and other languages will help people in other countries to gain a more objective and more rounded understanding of China, of its people, of its past and present, and of the spiritual world of contemporary Chinese. Such understanding should be conducive to promoting equal dialogue between China and other countries and exchanges between different civilizations.

The selection, explanation, and translation of these concepts have been made possible thanks to the support of the Ministry of Education, China International Publishing Group, the Central Compilation and Translation Bureau, Peking University, Renmin University of China, Wuhan University, and Beijing Foreign Studies University, as well as the support of renowned scholars in China and abroad, including Florence Chia-ying Yeh, Li Xueqin, Zhang Qizhi, Lin Wusun, Lou Yulie, and Wang Ning.

The idea of compiling key concepts in Chinese thought and culture represents an innovation and the project calls much research and effort both in connotation and denotation. Furthermore, an endeavor like this has not been previously attempted on such a large scale. Lack of precedents means there must remain much room for improvement. Therefore, we welcome comments from all readers in the hope of better fulfilling this task.

December 11, 2021

目录
Contents

1. àimín 爱民
   Love the People 1
2. àirényǐdé 爱人以德
   Love the People in Accordance with Rules of Moral Conduct 3
3. ānjū-lèyè 安居乐业
   Live in Peace and Work in Contentment 4
4. bǎixì 百戏
   Baixi (All Performing Arts) 6
5. biānsàishī 边塞诗
   Frontier Poetry 7
6. biāojǔ-xìnghuì 标举兴会
   Distinctiveness and Spontaneity 9
7. bó'ài 博爱
   Extensive Love to Benefit All People 11
8. bùzhàn'érshèng 不战而胜
   Win Without Resorting to War 13
9. bùzhànzàiwǒ 不战在我
   Do not Engage the Enemy If Victory Is Not Guaranteed 14
10. cānyàn 参验
    Cross-checking and Verification 16

11 cānglǐn shí ér zhī lǐjié 仓廪实而知礼节
   When the Granaries Are Full, the People Follow Appropriate
   Rules of Conduct. 17

12 Chángchéng 长城
   The Great Wall 19

13 chàngshén 畅神
   Free Flow of One's Mind 21

14 chéngrén 成人
   Complete Man 23

15 chóngběn-jǔmò 崇本举末
   Revere the Fundamental and Keep the Specific Unchanged 25

16 chóngběn-xīmò 崇本息末
   Revere the Fundamental and Dismiss the Specific 26

17 《Chūnqiū》 bǐfǎ 春秋笔法
   The Style of *The Spring and Autumn Annals* 27

18 dàzhàngfu 大丈夫
   Great Man 29

19 dāngrén-bùràng 当仁不让
   When Facing an Opportunity to Exercise Benevolence,
   Do Not Yield. 31

20 dérénzhěxīng, shīrénzhěbēng 得人者兴，失人者崩
He Who Obtains the Support of the People Will Rise; He Who Loses the Support of the People Will Come to Ruin. 32

21 diǎntiě-chéngjīn 点铁成金
Turning a Crude Poem or Essay into a Literary Gem 34

22 fǎ 法
Law / Dharma 36

23 fǎn zhě dào zhī dòng 反者道之动
The Only Motion Is Returning. 38

24 fàn'ài 泛爱
Broad Love Extending to All 39

25 fēimìng 非命
Rejection of Fatalism 41

26 gé 格
Examine / Study 42

27 gōngdiào 宫调
Gongdiao (Musical Modes) 44

28 gōngzhèng 公正
Fair / Just 46

29 gǔwén yùndòng 古文运动
Classical Prose Movement 47

13

30 hánxù 含蓄
　　Subtle Suggestion 50

31 hányǒng 涵泳
　　Be Totally Absorbed (in Reading and Learning) 52

32 hànyuèfǔ 汉乐府
　　Yuefu Poetry 54

33 háofàngpài 豪放派
　　The *Haofang* School / The Bold and Unconstrained School 56

34 hào zhàn bì wáng, wàng zhàn bì wēi
　　好战必亡，忘战必危
　　Those Who Like to Go to War Will Perish; Those Who Forget War Will Be in Danger. 59

35 héwéiguì 和为贵
　　Harmony Is Most Precious. 61

36 huānghán 荒寒
　　Grim and Desolate 62

37 Huáng Hé 黄河
　　The Yellow River 64

38 huìmín 惠民
　　Benefit the People 65

39 jī 几
　　Ji (Omen) 67

14

40 jǐsuǒbùyù, wùshīyúrén 己所不欲，勿施于人
   Do Not Do to Others What You Do Not Want Others to Do to You. 68

41 Jiàn'ān fēnggǔ 建安风骨
   The Jian'an Literary Style 69

42 jiěbì 解蔽
   Clear the Mind of Enigmas..71

43 jīngqì 精气
   Vital Energy 73

44 kèjǐ-fùlǐ 克己复礼
   Restrain Yourself and Follow Social Norms 74

45 kūdàn 枯淡
   Dry Plainness 75

46 kuángjuàn 狂狷
   Proactive Versus Prudent 77

47 lǐqù 理趣
   Philosophical Substance Through Artistic Appeal 78

48 liǎngyí 两仪
   Two Modes...80

49 lóng 龙
   Chinese Dragon 82

50 luànshìzhīyīn 乱世之音
   Music of an Age of Disorder..83

51 mínxīn 民心
Will of the People 85

52 mínxīn-wéiběn 民心惟本
The People's Will Is the Foundation of the State.................87

53 mín yǐ shí wéi tiān 民以食为天
Food Is of Primary Importance to the People......................88

54 mínzhǔ 民主
Lord of the People / Democracy 90

55 qīngcí-lìjù 清词丽句
Refreshing Words and Exquisite Expressions....................92

56 rénmín-àiwù 仁民爱物
Have Love for the People, and Cherish All Things.............93

57 sānbùxiǔ 三不朽
Set Moral Examples, Perform Great Deeds, and Spread Noble Ideas...95

58 shānshuǐshī 山水诗
Landscape Poetry 96

59 shàngtóng 尚同
Conform Upwardly 98

60 shàngxián 尚贤
Exalt the Worthy...100

61 shēngshēng 生生
Perpetual Growth and Change 101

62 shèngtángzhīyīn 盛唐之音
Poetry of the Prime Tang Dynasty 102

63 shìdézhěchāng, shìlìzhěwáng 恃德者昌，恃力者亡
Those Who Rely on Virtue Will Thrive; Those Who Rely on
Force Will Perish. 105

64 sìxiàng 四象
Four Images 107

65 Tàikāng tǐ 太康体
The Taikang Literary Style 109

66 tì 悌
Fraternal Duty 110

67 tiānjīng-dìyì 天经地义
Natural Rules and Orderliness 112

68 tiānshí dìlì rénhé 天时地利人和
Opportune Time, Geographic Advantage, and Unity of the People 113

69 tiānxià-wéigōng 天下为公
The World Belongs to All. 114

70 tiányuánshī 田园诗
Idyllic Poetry 116

71 wǎnyuēpài 婉约派
The *Wanyue* School / The Graceful and Restrained School 117

17

72 wángguózhīyīn 亡国之音
Music of a Failing State 119

73 wúwéi'érzhì 无为而治
Rule Through Non-action 120

74 wùhuà 物化
Transformation of Things 122

75 xīkūn tǐ 西昆体
The Xikun Poetic Style 123

76 xiāngyuàn 乡愿
Hypocrite 125

77 xiào 孝
Filial Piety 126

78 xīnzhāi 心斋
Pure State of the Mind 127

79 xíngjǐ-yǒuchǐ 行己有耻
Conduct Oneself with a Sense of Shame 129

80 xìng'è 性恶
Human Nature Is Evil. 130

81 xìngshàn 性善
Human Nature Is Good. 131

82 xuányánshī 玄言诗
Metaphysical Poetry 133

18

83 《Xuǎn》tǐ, xuǎntǐ 选体
Xuanti Poetry / Poetry in Prince Zhaoming's Favorite Style 134

84 yífēng-yìsú 移风易俗
Change Social Practices and Customs... 136

85 yǐzhàn-zhǐzhàn 以战止战
Use War to Stop War... 137

86 yǐnyìshī 隐逸诗
Recluse Poetry 139

87 Yǒngmíng tǐ 永明体
The Yongming Poetic Style.. 140

88 yǒngshǐshī 咏史诗
Poetry on History 142

89 yuánhēng-lìzhēn, yuán-hēng-lì-zhēn 元亨利贞
Yuanheng Lizhen 143

90 yuàncì 怨刺
Resentment and Sting 145

91 yuēdìng-súchéng 约定俗成
Established Through Popular Usage / Accepted Through Common Practice 146

92 yuè 乐
Yue (Music) 147

93 zhèngguìyǒuhéng 政贵有恒
Stability Is the Key to Governance. 149

94 Zhèngshǐ tǐ 正始体
The Zhengshi Literary Style 150

95 zhìnèi-cáiwài 治内裁外
Handling Internal Affairs Takes Precedence over External Affairs. 151

96 zhìshìzhīyīn 治世之音
Music of an Age of Good Order 153

97 zhōnghé 中和
Balanced Harmony 154

98 zìshēng 自生
Spontaneous Generation 155

99 zìyóu 自由
Acting Freely / Freedom 156

100 zuòwàng 坐忘
Forget the Difference and Opposition Between Self and
the Universe 158

术语表 List of Concepts 160

中国历史年代简表 A Brief Chronology of Chinese History 166

àimín 爱民

Love the People

仁爱民众；爱护百姓。它不仅是治国者应该具有的对百姓的一种情怀，而且是治国理政必须遵循的重要原则。古人认为，治国者应该通过具体的政策、措施，使民众获利，安居乐业，免受痛苦和无端侵害。这也是治国者获得民众尊崇的前提或基础。"爱民"不仅是重要的政治理念，而且延伸到军事领域，成为兴兵作战的重要原则。依照这个原则，敌我双方的民众都应该受到爱护。它是中华"民本""仁义"思想的展现。

This term means to love and care for the common people. This is not only a sentiment which those who govern should have for the common people, but also an important principle which must be adhered to in governance. The ancient Chinese believed that those who govern should use specific policies and measures to benefit the people and enable them to live and work peacefully, free from sufferings and unwarranted infringements. This is the precondition or basis for those who govern to win the respect of the people. "Loving the people" was not only an important political concept – it also extended to the military sphere and became an important principle when raising armies to make war. According to this principle, the people of both one's own side and that of the enemy should receive caring love. This is a manifestation of the Chinese thinking "people first" and "benevolence and righteousness."

引例 Citations：

◎文王问太公曰："愿闻为国之大务，欲使主尊人安，为之奈何？"太公曰："爱民而已。"文王曰："爱民奈何？"太公曰："利而勿害，成而勿败，生而

勿杀，与而勿夺，乐而勿苦，喜而勿怒。"（《六韬·文韬·国务》）
（周文王问姜太公："我想知道治理国家最重要的事情是什么，要使君主得到尊崇、民众得到安宁，应该怎么办呢？"姜太公说："只要爱民就可以了。"周文王问："怎样爱民呢？"姜太公说："使民众获利而不去妨碍他们，帮助民众成事而不去毁坏他们，利于民众生存而不去伤害他们，给予民众实惠而不是从他们手中夺走，使民众快乐而不是使他们痛苦，使民众高兴而不是使他们愤怒。"）

King Wen of Zhou asked Jiang Taigong, "I would like to ask: what are the most important things in governing a country that must be done for the ruler to enjoy respect and the people to have peace?" Jiang Taigong replied, "Just love the people." King Wen asked, "How does one love the people?" Jiang Taigong said, "Allow the people to gain profits and do not obstruct them; help the people achieve successes and do not ruin them; let the people live and do not harm them; give the people benefits and do not take them; bring the people joy and not suffering; make the people happy and not angry." (*The Six Strategies*)

◎古者以仁为本、以义治之之谓正。……战道：不违时，不历民病，所以爱吾民也；不加丧，不因凶，所以爱夫其民也；冬夏不兴师，所以兼爱其民也。（《司马法·仁本》）
（古人以仁爱为根本、以治军合乎道义为正道。……战争的原则是：不在农忙时兴兵，不在民众流行疫病时兴兵，为的是爱护自己的民众；不趁敌国有国丧时发动战争，不趁敌国有灾荒时发动战争，为的是爱护敌国的民众；不在冬夏两季兴兵，为的是爱护敌我双方的民众。）

The ancient people considered benevolent love to be the foundation of society, and the use of force in ethical ways as the proper way… The principles of warfare are to not assemble an army during the harvest season or when there is an epidemic among the people, because you love your own people; to not start a war when the enemy state is in mourning or has a natural disaster, because you love its people; to not assemble an army during the winter or summer, because you love both your people and your enemy's people. (*The General Commander's Treatise on War*)

àirényǐdé 爱人以德

Love the People in Accordance with Rules of Moral Conduct

爱他人要以合乎道德规范为原则，不能无原则地偏私偏爱、迁就纵容。"德"即道德规范，也指人的道德品行，它是维护良好社会秩序的内在依据。"爱人"属于个人层面的情感，而"德"则是全社会应共同遵守的规范。"爱人"若不"以德"，则既违背了社会的共同规范，也损害爱人者和被爱者的个人品德。"爱人以德"体现了尊崇道义、注重社会秩序及公共利益的精神。

Love of others must follow the rules of moral conduct, and not be unprincipled, selfish or indulgent. *De* (德) here refers to moral behavior and consciousness, and is the foundation for upholding proper social order. Loving the people is on a personal emotional level, while morality is a set of commonly accepted rules of social conduct. If not grounded in morality, loving the people will go against the common social norms, and harm the integrity of both giver and receiver. The term expresses a spirit of respect for morality, social order, and common good.

引例 Citations：

◎曾子曰："……君子之爱人也以德，细人之爱人也以姑息。吾何求哉？吾得

正而毙焉斯已矣。"(《礼记·檀弓上》)

(曾子说:"……君子爱人要遵循道德规范,小人爱人则是一味迁就求得安宁。我还求什么呢?死的时候都能合乎规范,这已经心满意足了。")

Zengzi said, "...The man of virtue follows the codes of moral conduct when loving others, while the petty person is indulgent for the sake of peace. What do I wish for? I shall be more than satisfied that by the time I die I will have followed all the codes of conduct." (*The Book of Rites*)

◎君子爱人以德,不可徇情废礼。(褚人获《隋唐演义》第二十三回)

(君子爱人要遵循道德规范,不能曲从私情而坏了规矩。)

The man of virtue follows the rules of moral conduct when loving others, and does not break them for purely personal reasons. (Chu Renhuo: *Romance of the Sui and Tang Dynasties*)

ānjū-lèyè 安居乐业

Live in Peace and Work in Contentment

安定地生活,愉快地工作。"安居",安于居所,指平平安安地生活。"乐业",乐于本业,以自己的职守为乐,指快乐地从事自己的本职工作。形容国家、社会治理得非常好,天下太平无事,人们各得其所,各安生计,幸福快乐。它是普通民众所抱有的基本社会理想,也是有所作为的政治家、管理者所追求的社会治理的目标。作为政治理想,它体现着以民为本、注重民生的基本精神。

Live a stable life and work happily. *Anju* (安居) literally means a secure house and by extension living a happy life. *Leye* (乐业) means enjoying one's work. Together they refer to the general state of good governance, with peace prevailing and everyone in their proper place, satisfied with work and content with life. It is the longing of the common people as well as the goal of good governance. It is a people-oriented political aspiration centering on securing people's livelihood.

引例 Citations：

◎至治之极……民各甘其食，美其服，安其俗，乐其业。(《史记·货殖列传》引《老子》)

（治理国家的最高境界……是使民众觉得吃的饭很香甜，穿的衣服很漂亮，习惯于他们的习俗，乐于他们所从事的行业。）

The highest state of good governance is one in which people feel satisfied with their food, clothes, willingly observe social norms, and love their trade. (*Laozi*, as cited in *Records of the Historian*)

◎普天之下，赖我而得生育，由我而得富贵，安居乐业，长养子孙，天下晏然，皆归心于我矣。(仲长统《理乱篇》，见《后汉书·仲长统传》)

（普天下的人，依赖我而得以生存生长，因为我而得以享受富贵，安于居所，乐于本职，养育子孙，天下太平，那么人们就都会真心诚意地归附于我了。）

If I can ensure that all the people under heaven survive and develop, are well-off, live in peace and work in contentment, and raise their children in a secure world, then they will willingly pledge allegiance to me. (Zhong Changtong: On Governance and Turmoil)

bǎixì 百戏

Baixi (All Performing Arts)

中国古代歌舞杂技表演的总称。包括武术、魔术、驯兽、歌舞、滑稽戏表演，及空中走绳、吞刀、踏火等各种杂技，内容丰富，形式多样，表演比较自由而随意，追求娱乐效果，具有民间性和通俗性。汉代开始流行，随着各民族的文化交流与融汇，乐舞杂技表演形式也不断融合、丰富，"百"是表示其种类繁多。南北朝以后其义同于"散乐"。唐代进一步盛行。宋代以后，散乐侧重指文人创作、艺人表演的歌舞、戏剧，百戏则相当于民间杂技。有时，统治者会因为百戏耽误正业甚至影响风气而颁布禁令。总的来说，百戏孕育了歌舞、戏剧等高雅艺术，留下了中国杂技这一非物质文化遗产，丰富了人们的精神文化生活。

It's a generic term in history for performing arts, including martial arts, magic, taming animals, song and dance, farce, tightrope walking, knife swallowing, walking on fire, and other acrobatic performances. Such performing arts were diverse in both form and content and the performance could easily take place, the only criterion being to entertain the popular audience. Such performances began in Han times, and as culture and art forms from different ethnic groups were slowly integrated into local practice, performing arts and acrobatics came to be increasingly diversified. The term *baixi* (百戏) literally means "a hundred forms of performances," and suggests, different kinds of performing arts. After the Southern and Northern Dynasties another term, *sanyue* (散乐), became synonymous with *baixi*. During the Tang Dynasty the performing arts became even more popular. In Song times *sanyue* came to refer mainly to song and dance performances or operas created by men of letters; while *baixi* came to mean principally acrobatic shows by folk artists. At times the authorities would impose a ban on *baixi*, believing that such performing arts exerted a bad influence on social customs. Still it is fair to say that *baixi* gave birth to highbrow song and dance as well as operas. It turned acrobatics into a form of intangible cultural heritage, enriching the cultural life of the people.

引例 Citation：

◎秦汉已来，又有杂伎，其变非一，名为百戏，亦总谓之散乐。（郭茂倩《乐府诗集》卷五十六引《唐书·乐志》）

（自秦汉以后，又加入了各种杂技，演变出的种类很多，总称为"百戏"，也总称为"散乐"。）

From the Qin and Han dynasties onward, there appeared different kinds of acrobatic shows and a great variety of performing arts, which were referred to as *baixi*, and were also called *sanyue*. (*The History of the Tang Dynasty*, as cited in Guo Maoqian: *Collection of Yuefu Poems*)

biānsàishī 边塞诗

Frontier Poetry

一种以塞外风光、边境战事及戍边生活为主要创作题材的诗歌流派。其作品或描绘奇异鲜明的塞外风光，或反映惨烈的战争场景与艰苦的戍边生活，有些则重点刻画戍边将士们的离别、思乡、报国之情或其配偶之闺怨及对前方亲人的思念等。边塞诗往往反映作者对战争的深切感受和思考，表现出个体生命价值与时代精神之间的一种张力。边塞诗以唐代为主，之后虽也有边塞之作，但规模与气象远不能与唐代相比。

Poems of this kind depicted frontier scenery as well as fighting along the northern border area and the life of soldiers garrisoned there. These poems described the scenic splendor north of the Great Wall, fierce war scenes, or hardships endured by frontier guards. Some of the works were about soldiers' agony caused by long separation from families and about their homesickness, but many such poems also extolled their patriotism. Some of the works voiced the longing for reunion of women left at home when husbands and sons went to the frontier. Frontier poems showed the poets' attitude towards and reflections on war, highlighting the tension between valuing individual lives and the need to respond to call to duty. The most compelling frontier poems were written in the Tang Dynasty. Frontier poems of later generations could not rival the powerful expression of Tang frontier poems.

引例 Citation：

◎盛唐诸公五言之妙，多本阮籍、郭璞、陶潜……边塞之作则出鲍照、吴筠（yún）也。唐人于六朝，率揽其菁华、汰其芜蔓，可为学古者之法。（王士禛《居易录》卷二十一）

（盛唐诗人们的五言诗，其精妙之处多取法于阮籍、郭璞、陶渊明等人的作品……而边塞诗则是学习鲍照、吴筠的作品。唐代诗人于六朝人的作品中，多能采撷它们的精华而去除它们芜杂枝蔓的毛病，这可以作为向古人学习的典范。）

Five-character-a-line poems written during the prime of the Tang Dynasty emulated the poetic style of Ruan Ji, Guo Pu, and Tao Yuanming, whereas frontier poems in this period were more influenced by Bao Zhao and Wu

Yun. Tang poets drew inspiration from the poetry of the Six Dynasties while discarding its defects of random extension and disorderliness. Their poems were therefore representative of classical poetry that we should learn from. (Wang Shizhen: *Records of a Secure and Peaceful Life*)

biāojǔ-xìnghuì 标举兴会

Distinctiveness and Spontaneity

亦作"兴会标举"。"标举"有"标明、突出"之义，后来引申出"鲜明、高超、独特"等众多含义。"会"是会聚，"兴会"是创作主体为外物所激发的创作状态及由此产生的丰富的心理感悟，是文学创作时灵感勃发而自然生成的浓厚兴致与意趣。"标举兴会"指文学创作中由"兴"所生发的丰富的心理感悟与情感特征，亦指作品中所呈现的浓厚而强烈的兴致与意趣。"标举兴会"既是一个文学批评术语，也是一种创作理念，它与崇尚自然、反对造作的写作态度相对应，推崇创作者的才华与激情，强调直觉基础上的自由想象和灵感勃发状态下的自由创造。

Also "spontaneity and distinctiveness." *Biaoju* (标举) originally meant "to mark out or stand out." It later extended to mean "superior, unique, distinctive, and outstanding." *Hui* (会) means "to get together." *Xinghui* (兴会) refers to one's passionate creative state and rich perceptions sparked by an object, and keen, naturally-inspired interest and charm in literary creation. The term, as a whole, indicates distinctive, spontaneous perceptions and emotions in literary creation, and intense interest and charm possessed by literary work. It is both a term of literary criticism and a concept of literary creation. Opposing false sentimentality, the term holds in esteem spontaneity, writers' talents and enthusiasm, and emphasizes free imagination based on intuition and free creation in a state of bursting inspirations.

引例 Citations：

◎灵运之兴会标举，延年之体裁明密，并方轨前秀，垂范后昆。（《宋书·谢灵运传论》）

（谢灵运的诗作意旨鲜明、情致高超，颜延之的诗作结构严谨、语言明晰，他们都取法于前代作家的优秀传统，成为后辈写作的典范。）

The spontaneity and distinctiveness of Xie Lingyun's poems as well as the closely-knitted structure and lucidity of Yan Yanzhi's poems, which both draw inspiration from poets before them, have stimulated poets of later time. (*The History of Song of the Southern Dynasties*)

◎一用兴会标举成诗，自然情景俱到。（王夫之《明诗评选》卷六）

（只要将直觉感受到的鲜明物象与灵感激发的独特感悟写成诗，自然有情有景，情景交融。）

A poem with spontaneity and distinctiveness will automatically blend one's sentiments and the natural setting. (Wang Fuzhi: *A Selection of Ming Poetry with Commentary*)

◎原夫创始作者之人，其兴会所至，每无意而出之，即为可法可则。……情偶至而感，有所感而鸣，斯以为风人之旨。（叶燮《原诗·内篇下》）

（推究诗歌的创作者，当兴会来临时，往往在无意间写出了至美的作品，这些作品即成为后世学习的典范。……心中的情偶然与外在的物相感，自然要将心中所感说出来，这就是诗人创作的本旨。）

A careful examination shows that a poet, when inspired, creates excellent works without knowing it. Such poems will thus become a model for future generations to emulate… When the poet's inner feelings interact with the external world, he naturally has the urge to express them. That is what poetry writing is all about. (Ye Xie: *Studies on the Purpose of Poetic Writing*)

bó'ài 博爱

Extensive Love to Benefit All People

广泛地爱，惠及所有的人。"博"即广泛、广大；"爱"即"惠"，惠及众人。古人认为，"安民则惠"（使民众安定生活就是惠），"爱"是"仁"的体现，而"仁"则是与人亲密。"博爱"犹言爱民、惠民，首先是一种执政理念，意在使国家的制度、法令、政策、措施的受益面尽可能最大化，使更多的人得到好处。它也指与众人亲密相处、友善相待、相互扶助的一种社会伦理、个人品格或情怀。

Bo (博) means extensive, wide; *ai* (爱) is synonymous with *hui* (惠) which means benefit to all. Ancient Chinese believed that ensuring the people a life of peace and security is *hui*. Love in turn is an expression of *ren* (仁), or benevolence, which is based on close human relationships. The term applies primarily to a concept of governance of "love for and benefit to the people," as demonstrated through its systems, laws, policies, and measures which should be as inclusive as possible. The term also refers to a kind of social morality and personal integrity based on harmonious engagement with others, goodwill, and mutual help.

引例 **Citations**：

◎先王见教之可以化民也，是故先之以博爱，而民莫遗其亲；陈之以德义，而民兴行……（《孝经·三才》）

（从前的贤明君主发现教育可以感化民众，所以先倡导博爱，民众因此没有遗弃双亲的；向民众讲述道德、礼义，民众于是起而遵行……）

Wise rulers in the past discovered that education could change people for the better so they advocated extensive love, and consequently no people abandoned their parents. They taught people about morality and rules of conduct, and consequently they all acted accordingly… (*Classic of Filial Piety*)

◎人君之道，清净无为，务在博爱，趋在任贤……（刘向《说苑·君道》）

（君主的治国理念或原则，在于顺其自然、不随便干预，努力惠及更多的人，努力任用有才德的人……）

The principles of a ruler should be to govern according to natural laws without unduly interfering, to benefit as many people as possible, and to select the talented and upright for office… (Liu Xiang: *Garden of Stories*)

◎博爱之谓仁，行而宜之之谓义，由是而之焉之谓道，足乎己无待于外之谓德。（韩愈《原道》）

（广爱众人就叫做"仁"，践行"仁"而行为合宜就叫做"义"，遵循"仁义"而前行就叫做"道"，无需借助外力达到自身完满就叫做"德"。）

To have a broad love for humans is benevolence, to implement benevolence and behave in the correct way is to have righteousness, and to act with benevolence and righteousness is to attain the proper way. To achieve a consummate personal state without outside intervention is to attain virtue. (Han Yu: The Origins of Dao)

bùzhàn'érshèng 不战而胜

Win Without Resorting to War

不用交战就已战胜敌人。源于古代著名的军事家孙武。孙武提出，最高明的用兵方略是"不战而屈人之兵"，方法有二：其一"伐谋"，挫败敌方的计谋，使敌人无计可施；其二"伐交"，破坏敌方的外交，使敌人孤立无援。由此造成敌必败、我必胜的战略态势，最终迫使敌人屈服。这是一种融政治、军事、外交于一体的大军事观，为历代有作为的军事家所推崇。时至今日，这一思想被广泛运用于国际关系、企业"商战"等众多领域。其核心是：做好自己，搞好联合。

This saying comes from Sunzi, the well-known military strategist, who said that the best military strategy is "to defeat the enemy without going to war." He listed two ways for achieving this: 1) the use of stratagems to foil the enemy's plans; 2) the use of diplomacy to totally isolate the enemy. The opponent is thus forced into a hopeless situation and compelled to submit. This is an over-arching vision of military strategy that combines politics, force, and diplomacy, and has been the ideal of generations of successful commanders. This thinking is prevalent up to the present day in international relations, "business wars," and other areas. At its heart is the dictum "build yourself and form alliances."

引例 Citation：

◎百战百胜，非善之善者也；不战而屈人之兵，善之善者也。故上兵伐谋，其次伐交，其次伐兵，其下攻城。攻城之法，为不得已。(《孙子·谋攻》)

（百战百胜，并不是最高明的用兵谋略；不用交战就使敌人屈服，才是最高明的用兵谋略。所以用兵的上策是挫败敌方的计谋，其次是破坏敌方的外交，再次是攻打敌方的军队，最下策是进攻敌方的城邑。攻城是不得已采取的办法。）

Winning every battle is not the wisest use of force. Making the enemy surrender without fighting is the best military strategy. The preferred way is to foil the enemy's plans, the next best to use diplomacy, failing that to attack the enemy's forces, and the least desirable is to assault the enemy's cities. Assaulting cities is a last resort when all else has failed. (*The Art of War*)

bùzhànzàiwǒ 不战在我

Do not Engage the Enemy If Victory Is Not Guaranteed.

　　若无胜算就不与敌人交战。是否交战取决于我，而不可受制于敌。这是古人提出的一种军事思想。"不战"并非消极避战。它的意思是说：当形势不利于我而利于敌的时候，我应避免与敌正面交锋，尤其要避免战略决战；不能因敌之动而仓促交战或被动应战，而应以持久防御使敌疲惫，同时设法调动敌人，迫敌露出破绽，然后乘隙出击、反攻，战而胜之。它强调的是在战争中要牢牢掌握主动权，不打无把握之仗。

To fight or not to fight is one's own decision, not the enemy's. This is a principle of military operations proposed by ancient Chinese. "Not to engage the enemy" does not mean passively avoiding confrontation, but means to avoid direct confrontation when the situation favors the enemy. One should not rush or be forced into confrontation just to respond to an enemy's move. Instead, opt for a sustained defense to wear the enemy out and move them in a way that forces them to reveal their vulnerabilities. Then seize the opportunity to attack or counter-attack and win the battle. This concept emphasizes the importance of taking control in waging a war and advises against fighting when victory is not assured.

引例 Citations：

◎故善战者，致人而不致于人。(《孙子·虚实》)
（所以善于指挥作战的人，能调动敌人而不为敌人所调动。）

Therefore, a competent commander can move around the enemy instead of being moved. (*The Art of War*)

◎孙武云："我不欲战者，画地而守之，敌不得与我战者，乖其所之也。"敌有人焉，则交绥之间未可图也，故曰不战在我。(《李卫公问对》卷下)
（孙武说："我若不想交战，则我据地防御，敌人无法和我交战，从而迫使敌人改变其进攻意图。"敌兵中如果有厉害的人，则进退之间我没有取胜的把握，所以说若无胜算就不与敌人交战。）

Sunzi said, "If I do not want to engage, then I take a position to defend myself and make my enemy unable to engage me. Thus, I can force my enemy to change the intention of attack." I may not be able to win either by moving backward or forward if encountering a powerful enemy. That's why I say do not engage the enemy if victory is not guaranteed. (*Li Jing Answering Emperor Taizong of the Tang Dynasty*)

cānyàn 参验

Cross-checking and Verification

通过观察、比较获得验证，是检验认识与言论正确与否的一种方法。"参验"之法在先秦时期即屡被提及，韩非子（前280？—前233）对这一方法做出了较为深入的阐发。韩非子认为，要判断某一认识或言论的正确性，需要从天、地、物、人等多方面进行比较、检验，这就是"参验"。"参验"应注重认识或言论的实际功用。只有通过比较、检验而证明能够发挥实际功用的认识或言论才是正确的。如果不经"参验"就盲目加以肯定，是愚昧的做法。

One way to confirm whether one's assessments and opinions are correct is to verify them through observation and comparison. The method of cross-checking and verification was frequently mentioned in the pre-Qin period. Hanfeizi (280?-233 BC) expounded this method in detail. He believed that to determine whether something was correct or not, it was necessary to compare, check, and verify from various perspectives: from heaven, earth, objects, and human beings. In using this method, one should focus on the practical effects of assessments and opinions. Only such assessments and opinions that can be proven to produce real effects through comparison, cross-checking, and verification are correct. To blindly confirm something without cross-checking and verification is foolish.

引例 Citation：

◎循名实而定是非，因参验而审言辞。(《韩非子·奸劫弑臣》)

(依循名号与实体是否一致而确定是非，依据参验的结果而审察言辞是否正确。)

Right or wrong, it should be determined by whether a name conforms to an entity or matter. Whether one's opinions are correct or not should be judged by cross-checking and verification. (*Hanfeizi*)

cānglǐn shí ér zhī lǐjié 仓廪实而知礼节

When the Granaries Are Full, the People Follow Appropriate Rules of Conduct.

粮仓充实了，人们才会懂得礼节。出自《管子·牧民》："仓廪实则知礼节，衣食足则知荣辱。""仓廪"是古代储藏米谷的地方或设施。"仓廪实""衣食足"指粮食储备充足，民众不愁吃穿，代指人们生产、生活所需的物质条件非常充足，即物质文明发展到一定阶段；"礼节""荣辱"指社会的礼仪规矩和内心的道德准则，包括了制度文明和精神文明。这句话揭示了物质文明和制度文明、精神文明之间的关系：物质文明是制度文明和精神文明产生的基础和条件，制度文明和精神文明是物质文明发展到一定阶段的产物。如果民众的基本生活条件都得不到保障，即使有良好的制度也难为人们所遵循，人们的精神品格也不可能得到提升。在任何时候，物质文明建设都应当成为治国理政的基本要务。这是一种非常务实的治国理念。

The full quote from *Guanzi* reads: "When the granaries are full, the people follow appropriate rules of conduct, and when there is enough to eat and wear, the people know honor and shame." Here "granaries" and "eat and wear" mean the material conditions of life, while "rules of conduct" and "honor and shame" represent the social and moral principles of a society, as well as the systems and spiritual culture that underpin it. The quote highlights the relationship between material life and morality, that is to say, the former is the basis for the latter, and morality and social norms are the product of a certain degree of material development. Without the basic assurances for life, the best systems will not be followed, and the moral standards of the people will remain low. At all times, governance should focus first on improving the material conditions of a society. This is a very practical concept of state governance.

引例 Citations：

◎故曰："仓廪实而知礼节，衣食足而知荣辱。"礼生于有而废于无。故君子富，好行其德；小人富，以适其力。渊深而鱼生之，山深而兽往之，人富而仁义附焉。(《史记·货殖列传》)
（所以 [管仲] 说："粮仓充实了，人们才能懂得礼节；衣食丰足了，人们才能分辨荣辱。"礼因生活条件的富足而建立，因生活条件的缺乏而废弃。因此，地位高的人富了，就会广泛推行道德；平民百姓富了，就会根据自己的力量遵行道德。水深了，鱼自然在那里生长；山深了，野兽自然奔向那里；人富了，仁义自然随之出现。）

So Guanzi said, "When the granaries are full, the people follow appropriate rules of conduct, and when there is enough to eat and wear, the people know honor and shame." Proper social norms emerge from sufficient conditions for life, and disappear when conditions are absent. That is why when people of high status become wealthy, they will widely advocate moral standards, and when ordinary people become wealthy they will behave in a moral way according to their means. Where the water is deep, fish will congregate; where the mountains are vast, wild animals will gather; when people are well off, a society of compassion and righteousness will appear. (*Records of the Historian*)

◎管子曰："仓廪实而知礼节。"民不足而可治者，自古及今，未之尝闻。……夫积贮者，天下之大命也。苟粟多而财有余，何为而不成？以攻则取，以守则固，以战则胜。怀敌附远，何招而不至？（贾谊《论积贮疏》，见《汉书·食货志》）

（管仲说："粮仓充实了，人们才能懂得礼节。"百姓的基本生活条件不足而能治理得很好，从古到今，还没听说过。……积蓄财物、贮存粮食是关系国计民生的大事。如果粮食多了、财富充裕了，那干什么事不能成功呢？用来进攻则攻无不取，用来防守则固若金汤，用来作战则无往而不胜。招抚敌方、远方的人归顺，谁会不来呢？）

Guanzi said, "When the granaries are full, the people follow appropriate rules of conduct." From time immemorial, no one has ever heard of successful governance when the people do not have enough to live on… Sufficient wealth and stores of grain are vital to the national economy and people's livelihood. What cannot be accomplished when granaries are stocked and coffers are full? Such a ruler will be victorious in offense, impregnable in defense, and invincible in war. To such a ruler, who would not come in submission, whether in surrender or through amnesty? (Jia Yi: *Memorial on Accumulation in Agriculture*)

Chángchéng 长城

The Great Wall

也称"万里长城"。由城墙、敌楼、关城、烽火台等多种建筑工事构成的完整的防御体系。公元前3世纪，秦王朝在统一中国后，为防御匈奴南侵，将战国时期燕、赵、秦等诸侯国修筑的长城连成一体并加固延长，修筑了西起临洮（今甘肃岷县）东至辽东（今辽宁省）、蜿蜒一万余里的长城。此后，两汉、北朝、隋等各代都曾在与北方游牧民族接壤的地带修筑长城。明朝是最后一个大修长城的朝代，自洪武（1368—1398）至万历（1573—1620）年间，先后修筑长城18次，今天人们看到的长城多是明长城。明长城西起嘉峪关，东至山海关，总长度为8851.8千米。长城是中国古代最伟大的军事防御工程，后世常用"长城"或"万里长城"比喻担负国家重任的人，长城还成为中华民族团结一心、众志成城、坚不可摧的一种文化象征。

The Great Wall, also known as the "10,000-*li* (5,000 kilometer) long Great Wall," was a complete defensive system consisting of walls, watchtowers, gated passes, and beacon towers. After unifying China in the 3rd century BC, the Qin Dynasty sought to ward off southward incursions of the northern nomadic tribes known as the Xiongnu by linking up and fortifying sections of the defense walls which had been built by the feudal states of Yan, Zhao, and Qin during the Warring States Period that had just ended. Extending about 10,000 *li*, the Great Wall wound its way from Lintao in the west (present day Minxian County, Gansu Province) to Liaodong in the east (present-day Liaoning Province). Later dynasties including the Western and Eastern Han, the Northern Dynasties, and the Sui Dynasty all added sections to the Great Wall in places abutting on northern nomadic tribal areas. The Ming Dynasty was the last Chinese dynasty to engage in extensive construction of the Great Wall, which was rebuilt 18 times between the reigns of Hongwu (1368-1398) and Wanli (1573-1620). A great part of the Great Wall that still stands today is from the Ming Dynasty. The Ming Great Wall extends from the Jiayu Pass in the west to the Shanhai Pass in the east, with a total length of 8851.8 km. The Great Wall is the greatest defense work built in ancient China. Later the term a "great wall" or a "10,000-*li* long great wall" often alludes to a person or a group of people who are a bulwark of the country. This term is also a symbol of fortitude and unity of the Chinese nation.

引例 Citations：

◎乃使蒙恬北筑长城而守藩篱，却匈奴七百余里，胡人不敢南下而牧马……（贾谊《过秦论》）

（[秦始皇]于是派遣蒙恬到北方修筑长城、镇守边境，使匈奴后退七百余里，使胡人不敢南下中原来牧马……）

The First Emperor of the Qin Dynasty then sent General Meng Tian north to build the Great Wall and guard the border. This forced the Xiongnu people to pull back over 700 *li*, no longer daring to go south to raise their horses… (Jia Yi: On the Shortcomings of the Qin)

◎吞珪既丧，坏了万里长城，国中精锐已尽，如何是好？（陈忱《水浒后传》第十二回）

（吞珪死了，国家的栋梁毁坏了，国中的精锐没有了，怎么办好呢？）

As Tian Gui is dead, the country's great wall has collapsed, and its elite are lost. What should we do? (Chen Chen: *Sequel to Outlaws of the Marsh*)

chàngshén 畅神

Free Flow of One's Mind

指精神与自然合一时所达到的自由舒畅的一种审美状态。特指欣赏山水画、山水诗时精神融入自然及物象的审美效应。南朝画家宗炳（375—443）在《画山水序》中指出，欣赏山水画可以领悟古代圣贤寄寓在山水中的哲理与乐趣，可以进入一种摒弃了一切外物和杂念的绝对虚无境界，它是一种全身心的极度愉悦和精神的最高自由。他提出这一术语，不仅揭示了山水画、山水诗及自然美的特殊审美功能，也反映了传统文学艺术对天人和谐、心灵和谐的价值追求。

The term describes a state of mind one achieves when appreciating an artwork, in which process one's inner feelings interact freely and joyfully with nature. In particular, it describes one's aesthetic experience of appreciating landscape paintings and landscape poems, when one feels absorbed with the natural scenes and images depicted. In his "On the Creation of Landscape Paintings," Zong Bing (375-443), painter of the Southern Dynasties, pointed out that by watching landscape paintings, one can appreciate the philosophy and pleasure which sages of past times drew from landscape. When doing so, one becomes oblivious to the external world and is totally free from worldly considerations, thus achieving full satisfaction of both body and mind. This term not only reveals the unique aesthetic function of landscape paintings, landscape poems, and natural beauty, but also demonstrates traditional literature and arts' pursuit of harmony between nature and man and between mind and heart.

引例 Citation：

◎圣贤映于绝代，万趣融其神思，余复何为哉？畅神而已。（宗炳《画山水序》）
（古代的圣贤已经通过想象与思考领略融汇了自然山水中的万般旨趣，我还需要做什么呢？只需体会畅神所带来的快乐就可以了。）

As sages of remote past already discovered the philosophical wisdom inherent in nature through imagination and contemplation, what more do I need to do now? All I have to do is relishing the joy when my mind interacts freely with the depicted landscape. (Zong Bing: On the Creation of Landscape Paintings)

chéngrén 成人

Complete Man

具备了健全德性与全面技能的人。在古人看来，"成人"的标志并不是年龄的增长所带来的身体的成熟，而是通过学习、修养获得了健全的德性和全面的技能。"成人"需要具备智慧、勇气，能够节制自己的欲望，并掌握各种技能，从而恰当地应对、处理生活中的各种事务，使自己的言行始终合于道义。

A complete man refers to a person of sound moral integrity who also has command of various skills that in ancient times were needed to deal with social life. In the view of the ancient Chinese, a complete man did not just mean that a man reached adulthood. It also meant that a person had acquired sound morals and the skills required to adapt to society. A complete man needed to have wisdom, courage, and self-restraint and also to have mastered the skills necessary to appropriately deal with all types of matters in life, so that his words and deeds met the requirements of moral principles and justice.

引例 Citations：

◎子路问成人。子曰："若臧武仲之知，公绰之不欲，卞庄子之勇，冉求之艺，文之以礼乐，亦可以为成人矣。"曰："今之成人者何必然？见利思义，见危授命，久要不忘平生之言，亦可以为成人矣。"(《论语·宪问》)

（子路请教何谓"成人"。孔子说："像臧武仲那样有智慧，像孟公绰那样寡欲，像卞庄子那样勇敢，像冉求那样有才艺，再用礼乐加以修饰，也就可以称为'成人'了。"又说："现在所说的'成人'何必一定这样？看到利益考虑是否正当，遇到危险肯付出生命，长久处于穷困仍不忘记平日的诺言，也可以说是'成人'了。"）

Zilu asked what qualities a complete man needed to have. Confucius said, "If someone has the wisdom of Zang Wuzhong, is free from covetousness as Meng Gongchuo is, has the courage of Bian Zhuangzi and the versatile skills of Ran Qiu, and is versed in rites and music, he can then be considered a complete man." Confucius then continued, "Now, what is the necessity of a complete man having all of these virtues? When faced with the temptation of self-interest, he thinks of the principle of justice. When at danger, he is ready to put his life at risk if necessary. When long in dire straits, he never forgets his past promises. Such a person can be said to be a complete man!" (*The Analects*)

◎德操然后能定，能定然后能应，能定能应，夫是之谓成人。(《荀子·劝学》)

（有道德操守然后能够志行坚定，志行坚定然后能够应对外物变化。能坚定，能应变，就可以称作"成人"了。）

With moral integrity, one can have strong willpower and are resolute in action; and with strong willpower and being resolute in action, one can respond to all changes with ease. Such a person can be called a complete man. (*Xunzi*)

chóngběn-jǔmò 崇本举末

Revere the Fundamental and Keep the Specific Unchanged

尊崇"本"以成就、保全"末",是对待"本""末"关系的一种方式。王弼(226—249)在解释老子思想时提出了"崇本举末"的思想,与"崇本息末"相对。这里的"本"指无形、无名者,即"道";"末"指自然之形、名。"崇本举末"即是要充分发挥"道"或"无"的作用,以使万物自然生成并得以保全。在政治领域,"崇本"特指君主以"道"为依据,施行无为之治。君主通过"崇本",使百姓依自然本性而生活。

This concept, as opposed to "revere the fundamental and dismiss the specific," originates in Wang Bi's (226-249) interpretation of Laozi. The fundamental, namely, Dao, is shapeless and nameless, while the specific refers to natural shapes and names. The term "revere the fundamental and keep the specific unchanged" means giving full rein to Dao and void so that the nature emerges and stays active. Politically, this term means a sovereign should govern on the basis of Dao and do nothing that goes against nature. He should revere the fundamental to ensure that the people can lead their lives as dictated by their inherent nature.

引例 Citation:

◎守母以存其子,崇本以举其末,则形名俱有而邪不生,大美配天而华不作。(王弼《老子注》)
(持守"道"以存养万物,尊崇"本"以成就、保全"末",则各种有形事物及其名称都能得以成就、保全而邪枉之事就不会产生,至美的事物与天匹配而浮华之事就不会兴起。）

Dao is adhered to in order to preserve all things. If the fundamental is revered and the specific is kept unchanged, then all tangible things will thrive and their names will remain, evil and wrong will not occur, great beauty will match the heaven, and vanity will not arise. (Wang Bi: *Annotations on Laozi*)

chóngběn-xīmò 崇本息末

Revere the Fundamental and Dismiss the Specific

尊崇"本"以止息"末",是对待"本""末"关系的一种方式。王弼（226—249）在解释老子思想时提出了"崇本息末"的思想,与"崇本举末"相对。这里的"本"指无形、无名者,即"道";"末"指人为造作的各种形、名。"崇本息末"即是要发挥"道"或"无"的作用以实现万物的自然,同时止息对人为造作的各种形名之物的追逐。在政治领域,"崇本"特指君主以"道"为依据,施行无为之治。君主通过"崇本",止息有关道德、礼法的教化以及各种浮华、虚伪的言行。

This term deals with the relationship between the fundamental and the specific. In interpreting Laozi, Wang Bi (226-249) put forth the idea of "revering the fundamental and dismissing the specific," as opposed to the idea of "revering the fundamental and keeping the specific unchanged." The fundamental here means Dao which is shapeless and nameless, while the specific refers to man-made things in various forms and names. The term "revere the fundamental and dismiss the specific" is meant to give full rein to Dao and void so as to maintain the inherent nature of all things and at the same time stop the pursuit of all kinds of man-made things in various forms and names. Politically, "revere the fundamental" means that a sovereign should govern on the basis of Dao and do nothing that goes against nature. At the same time, he should dismiss the rigid inculcation of moral values and rules and stop all false and pretentious rhetoric and behaviors.

引例 Citation：

◎故见素朴以绝圣智，寡私欲以弃巧利，皆崇本以息末之谓也。（王弼《老子指略》）

（因此呈现素朴的言行以杜绝圣、智的运用，减少对私欲的追求以摒弃巧、利的诱惑，这都是所说的"崇本息末"。）

Saying simple ideas and doing practical deeds rather than following sagacity and dogma, rejecting the pursuit of selfishness and resisting the temptation of trickery and vanity: this is what revering the fundamental and dismissing the specific is about. (Wang Bi: *An Outline of Laozi*)

《Chūnqiū》bǐfǎ 春秋笔法

The Style of *The Spring and Autumn Annals*

指编撰《春秋》的原则、方法。即用简洁的文字语句，婉转含蓄地表达一定的思想倾向和对历史人物及事件的褒贬和评判。也称"《春秋》书法""《春秋》笔削"，或说"一字褒贬""微言大义"。《春秋》相传为孔子（前551—前479）编撰，其主旨在于维护周朝礼制。书中没有用议论性文字正面阐明作者观点，而是通过对史实的简要记述，依据周礼选用一些有特殊含义的称呼或精妙字眼，婉转表达出对历史人物和事件的褒贬和评判。后来，它成为编撰史书的一个传统方法。

The style of *The Spring and Autumn Annals* is characterized by simple and concise language expressing ideas and commending or criticizing historical figures and events in an indirect way. The style is well known for "what is included or excluded has profound meanings." Also "every word in it reflects either approval or censure of the sage," and "subtle words carry profound meanings." Tradition has it that *The Spring and Autumn Annals* was edited by Confucius (551-479 BC) for the purpose of safeguarding the rites of the Zhou Dynasty. The text does not use argumentative language to express the author's views; instead, it tactfully expresses favorable and unfavorable views on historical figures and events by giving brief accounts using designations with special connotations or subtle expressions derived according to the rites of Zhou. Later on, this particular style became a traditional method of compiling history works.

引例 Citation：

◎故君子曰："《春秋》之称，微而显，志而晦，婉而成章，尽而不污，惩恶而劝善。非圣人谁能修之？"(《左传·成公十四年》)
(所以君子说："《春秋》用词细微而意义显豁，记述史实而内容幽深，婉转有致但顺理成章，直言其事绝不迂曲，惩戒邪恶而勉励向善。如果不是圣人，谁能够编写？")

Therefore the noble man said, "The style of *The Spring and Autumn Annals* is implicit but the meaning of the book is clear; it records both events and their profound significance. It is subtle yet logical, thorough yet not verbose. It chastises evil deeds and urges people to do good deeds. Who but a sage could have compiled this?" (*Zuo's Commentary on The Spring and Autumn Annals*)

dàzhàngfu 大丈夫

Great Man

一种对理想人格的称谓。是否能成为"大丈夫",并不是由个人的功业大小所决定的。评判"大丈夫"的根本标准,在于其对"道"的认知与坚守。不过由于各家对"道"的理解不同,因此对"大丈夫"的具体要求也有所差别。孟子(前372?—前289)强调"大丈夫"应有行道于天下的远大志向,并始终坚守道义,立身端正,不受外在事物的影响。老子则认为"大丈夫"应舍弃浮华的礼仪规范,以无为的方式回归朴实的自然状态。

This is a term used to describe someone of ideal moral quality. How much one achieves does not determine whether he can be called a great man. The criterion is whether or not a person can know and hold fast to Dao. Given that there are different interpretations of Dao, the specific requirements for a great man are also different. Mencius (372?-289 BC) stresses that a great man should have high aspirations to carry out Dao, adhere to moral integrity, stay upright, and his observation of Dao should not be influenced by external matters (as opposed to his inner world). Yet, another ancient Chinese philosopher Laozi believes that a great man should abandon ostentatious rites and norms, and return to the natural state through non-action.

引例 Citations:

◎居天下之广居,立天下之正位,行天下之大道;得志,与民由之;不得志,独行其道。富贵不能淫,贫贱不能移,威武不能屈,此之谓大丈夫。(《孟子·滕文公下》)

（居处在天下最广阔的住所，立身于天下最恰当的位置，遵行天下的大道。得志的时候，与民众一起遵行大道；不得志的时候，独自遵行其道。富贵不能使其行止失度，贫贱不能使其改变遵行的原则，权势不能使其屈服。这就是所谓的"大丈夫"。）

Living in the broad residence under heaven, staying in the proper place under heaven, one should observe the essential Dao under heaven. When having achieved one's ambitions, one should practice Dao along with the people; when failing to succeed in one's ambitions, one should observe Dao alone. Neither riches nor honors can corrupt him; neither poverty nor humbleness can make him swerve from his principles; neither threat nor force can subdue him. Such a person can be called a great man. (*Mencius*)

◎夫礼者，忠信之薄而乱之首。前识者，道之华而愚之始。是以大丈夫处其厚，不居其薄；处其实，不居其华。故去彼取此。（《老子·三十八章》）

（礼，标志着忠信的不足，是祸乱的端始。预设的种种规范，是道的浮华，是愚昧的端始。因此大丈夫处事敦厚，不为浇薄；处事朴实，不为浮华。所以舍弃浇薄浮华，而采取敦厚朴实的方式。）

Rites indicate a lack of loyalty and sincerity, and portend disorder. Preset norms are ostentatious representations of Dao and usher in stupidity. So a great man should be earnest rather than superficial, be simple rather than ostentatious. Such a person abandons everything superficial or ostentatious, and leads a simple and honest life. (*Laozi*)

dāngrén-búràng 当仁不让

When Facing an Opportunity to Exercise Benevolence, Do Not Yield.

面对正义之事，主动担当，不推让。"仁"本指仁德，是孔子（前551—前479）的最高理念，泛指一切应该做的事情，即符合道义、正义的事情。犹言"义不容辞""责无旁贷"。它弘扬的是一种以道义或正义为己任、勇于担当、勇于践行的主体精神。

This phrase means that one should behave ethically and never dodge one's responsibility. *Ren* (仁 benevolence) is the highest virtue upheld by Confucius (551-479 BC). In general, it refers to everything that is right to do, namely things compatible with moral principles and social justice. The term is similar in meaning to "committing oneself completely out of a sense of duty," and "feeling morally obliged." It promotes a positive attitude that takes safeguarding morality and justice as one's own responsibility and dares to shoulder and execute that responsibility.

引例 Citations：

◎子曰："当仁不让于师。"（《论语·卫灵公》）
（孔子说："面对着该做的仁义之事，即便是老师，也不和他谦让。"）

Confucius said, "When faced with an opportunity to be benevolent, one should not yield even to one's own teacher." (*The Analects*)

◎勇一也而用不同。有勇于气者，有勇于义者。君子勇于义，小人勇于气。（《二程外书》卷七）
（同样是"勇"，可以用在不同的地方。有的为了逞个人一时之气而表现"勇"，有的为了正义之事而显现"勇"。君子所以"勇"是为了道义，小人所以"勇"是为了逞个人一时之气。）

Courage can serve different purposes. Some people show courage at the spur of momentary emotions, while others do so for the sake of a just cause. A man of virtue becomes courageous when moral principles are at stake, whereas a petty man may be courageous in order to show off momentarily in front of others. (*More Writings of the Cheng Brothers*)

dérénzhěxīng, shīrénzhěbēng 得人者兴，失人者崩

He Who Obtains the Support of the People Will Rise; He Who Loses the Support of the People Will Come to Ruin.

得到人心或人才就会兴旺，失去人心或人才就会衰亡。"人"指民心、人心，也指人才。语出《史记·商君列传》。其含义有二：其一，民心、人心决定一个国家或政权的盛衰兴替。只有得到民心、顺应民意，才能保持国家或政权的兴盛不衰。这与"民心惟本""民惟邦本"的思想是一致的。其二，人才对国家、政权的兴盛与否起着至关重要的作用。只有识人、得人，任人唯贤，知人善任，才能成就大业，保持国家和政权的长治久安。得到人心与得到人才又相互关联：得人心，必能招致人才；得人才，必然赢得人心。大至国家、政权，小至机构、团队，在上位者都须遵从这一理念。

The term means that those who win the hearts of the people or get the service of the talented will rise while those who lose the hearts of the people or fail to get the talented people will perish. *Ren* (人) stands for people's hearts as well as people's talents. This saying, which comes from *Records of the Historian*, has two connotations. First, the rise and fall of a country or government depend on winning people's hearts. Only by winning people's hearts and responding to their wishes can a country or government continue to thrive. This is in accord with the philosophy that "the people's will is the foundation of the state" and "people are the foundation of the state." Second, talents are critical to the rise and fall of a country or government. Only by identifying and recruiting the most capable and most upright people, and by suitably employing them can a great cause be completed and a country and its government remain stable and secure. Winning people's hearts is closely related to attracting the talented. Winning people's hearts will eventually draw in the talented, and recruiting the talented will eventually help win people's hearts. All leaders, be they heads of states, groups or teams, should follow this notion of ruling.

引例 Citations：

◎政之所兴，在顺民心；政之所废，在逆民心。(《管子·牧民》)
(国家政权的兴盛在于顺应民心，国家政权的衰落在于违逆民心。)

A country will prosper when it goes along with people's wishes. It will fall if it goes against people's will. (*Guanzi*)

◎天下者无常乱，无常治，不善人在则乱，善人在则治。(《管子·小称》)
(天下没有长久的动乱，也没有长久的太平，如果品行不端的人当政，国家就会发生动乱；如果品行端正的人当政，国家就会太平。)

There is no lasting turmoil or peace in a country. Turmoil will ensue if a person of bad character is in power. On the other hand, peace will prevail if an upright person reigns. (*Guanzi*)

◎夫政理，得人则兴，失人则毁。(赵蕤《长短经·政体》)

（就治国理政而言，得到贤才事业就会兴盛，反之就会失败。）

With regard to governance, a nation that gets the service of the talented will thrive. Otherwise, it will go to ruin. (Zhao Rui: *On the Thoughts of Strategists*)

diǎntiě-chéngjīn 点铁成金

Turning a Crude Poem or Essay into a Literary Gem

指高明的作者用平常词句或化用前人的词句创造性地表达出神奇精妙的意蕴。亦指高手修改文章，善于从平凡文字中提炼出闪光点。北宋黄庭坚（1045—1105）沿袭刘勰（465？—520）的"宗经"思想，强调学习、揣摩经典作品的表达技巧，巧妙化用前人的词句，化平常、腐朽为神奇，使自己的文章主旨鲜明而又富有文采。此说推动了宋代及后世关于诗文创作手法的讨论。

The term "turning a crude poem or essay into a literary gem" means creatively expressing novel and exquisite meaning through the use of simple language or by transforming old phrases from past masters. The expression also can be used to describe the way that an accomplished man of letters edits writings. By minor adjustment, he can bring out the splendor in an otherwise ordinary piece. Huang Tingjian (1045-1105), a poet and scholar of the Northern Song Dynasty, valued and promoted literary critic Liu Xie's (465?-520) idea that classics offer excellent examples from which to learn, but he stressed the need to study and employ the expressive techniques found in classic masterpieces by cleverly transforming the words found there, altering common and hackneyed forms of "novelty" so as to impart to one's own writing freshness and literary style. In the

Song Dynasty and later, this theory gave rise to many debates about methods of creative writing in poetry.

引例 Citations：

◎古之能为文章者，真能陶冶万物，虽取古人之陈言入于翰墨，如灵丹一粒，点铁成金也。（黄庭坚《答洪驹父（fǔ）书》）

（古代那些擅长写作的大家，确实能够将各种文字和物象融为一体，即使是采用前人的陈旧辞句，也像用一颗灵丹就能点铁成金那样［表达出神奇精妙的意蕴］。）

In ancient times the most capable writers could render excellent images of virtually anything mentioned in their writing. Even if old expressions or sentences from former masters entered into their writing, they could transform them like an alchemist who, with a single touch, could turn lead into gold. (Huang Tingjian: Letter in Reply to Hong Jufu)

◎"椎床破面枨（chéng）触人，作无义语怒四邻。尊中欢伯见尔笑：我本和气如三春。"前两句本粗恶语，能煅炼成诗，真造化手，所谓点铁成金矣。（吴可《藏海诗话》）

（［有人醉酒后］"捶打坐床撕破脸面触犯他人，满嘴说些无情无义的话激怒四周的人。杯中的酒见到你们的丑态觉得可笑：'我'本是性情温和有如三春的饮品。"前两句本是很粗俗的话，能够锤炼成诗句，真是创意点化的高手，可以说是点铁成金了。）

"When drunk, you strike the bed to offend others, and vex your neighbors with vulgar language. The liquor in the cup laughs at you saying: I am a drink as gentle and warm as the spring weather." The first two sentences were crude, yet for you to transmute such material into a fine poem is true mastery. This is what is called a golden touch! (Wu Ke: *Canghai's Remarks on Poetry*)

fǎ 法

Law / Dharma

　　"法"的本义指刑罚，引申而指法律、法令和法律制度。在古代中国，"法"和"礼"都是对人行为的规范："礼"（礼教）旨在扬善，"法"（刑罚）旨在惩恶。古人认为，"法"虽由君王制定和颁布，但是君王和天下的人须共同遵守，它体现了法的正义性与公平性。公元前 536 年，郑国执政子产（？—前 522）将郑国的法律条文铸在象征诸侯权力的鼎上，史称"铸刑书"，这是中国历史上第一次向民众发布成文法。战国时期，产生了以商鞅（前 390？—前 338）、韩非子（前 280？—前 233）为代表的法家学说。"法"（dharma）又为佛教术语。在佛教典籍中，"法"主要有三种含义：其一，指真实的存在，即真知的对象。佛教认为日常事物都是依待各种条件合成的，表象所见悉皆不实，通过修行，可以观见其中不可再分的真实要素，包括物质、意识功能等要素上百种。其二，指如实的教导。它既是佛陀言说的教法，也是听法者应当实现的目标。这一观念与阿毗达摩之法相的具体含义虽然有别，却并不相违，因为对于真实的认识基于相应的教导。这些不仅是佛教知识体系的重要组成部分，也是实现解脱的基础。其三，指世间现象。不同于上述指向解脱的法，佛教典籍中亦有"诸法""万法"的说法，在最宽泛的意义上指世间一切现象，它们是不真实的。

The Chinese character *fa* (法), originally meaning "penalty," refers to the legal system consisting of laws, decrees, and regulations. In ancient China, both *fa* and *li* (礼 rite) set standards for individual behavior. In particular, rites rewarded virtue, while laws punished vice. It was generally accepted that while only a sovereign ruler had the right to enact and promulgate laws, everyone, be it a ruler or a subject, had to obey the laws. This point of view reflects the justice and fairness of law. In 536 BC, Zichan (?-522 BC), the chief minister in the State of Zheng, had the legal provisions cast on a bronze *ding*, a tripodal vessel that symbolized the power of the ducal ruler. Zichan's action, known as "casting the penal code," was the very first example of publishing a statute in Chinese history. The Warring States Period witnessed the rise of the Legalists such as Shang Yang (390?-338 BC) and Hanfeizi (280?-233 BC).

Fa (法) is also a Buddhist term. In scriptures, it is the Chinese equivalent of the Sanskrit word *dharma* with three shades of meaning. First, it refers to real being, which is the object of genuine knowledge. Buddhism argues that all things in daily life are produced through the concomitance of causes and conditions. In this sense, what one appears to see or know is unreal in nature. However, one can perceive the dharmas, the indivisible real elements beneath the surface, through mental practices. Indeed, there are more than a hundred types of the elements, such as substance and consciousness. Second, dharma can be defined as the Buddhist teachings. The teachings here not only refer to the words dictated by the Buddha but also what dharma-hearers receive and pursue. This point of view is different from the characteristics of dharma discussed in the *Abhidhamma Piṭaka* (Basket of Advanced Dharma). But they do not contradict each other, because both of them advocate that perception of reality be based on relevant teachings. For Buddhism as a whole, the teachings constitute a significant portion of its knowledge system; for all Buddhists, the teachings pave the way for their personal liberation. Third, dharma denotes the worldly phenomenon, which is clearly distinguishable from the previous meaning. In scriptures, *zhufa* (all dharmas) and *wanfa* (tens of thousands of dharmas) represent all worldly phenomena, unreal in nature, in the broadest sense.

引例 Citations：

◎法者，刑罚也，所以禁强暴也。(桓宽《盐铁论·诏圣》)
(法就是刑罚，是用来禁止强暴的。)

Laws are punishments for the purpose of prohibiting violence and crime.(Huan Kuan: *Discourses on Salt and Iron*)

◎夫礼禁未然之前，法施已然之后。(《史记·太史公自序》)
(礼的作用是阻止作恶之事发生，法则是在作恶之事发生之后进行惩罚。)

Rites are practiced before crimes can be committed, while laws as punishments are enforced afterwards. (*Records of the Historian*)

◎心、心所法亦非实我，不恒相续，待众缘故。(《成唯识论》卷一)
(意识和由意识产生的各种心智功能也都不是真实的自我，因为这些法都依待各种条件产生，并不能恒久持续。)

Neither mind nor its resulting mental factors belong to the real self. They cannot last permanently, because they are produced through the concomitance of various causes and conditions.(*Collected Commentaries to the Perfection of Consciousness-only*)

fǎn zhě dào zhī dòng 反者道之动

The Only Motion Is Returning.

"道"的运动就是向对立面的转化或复归。出自《老子》。老子认为，"道"是事物运动、变化的基本法则。这一法则的基本内涵即是"反"。"反"

包含两种不同的含义：其一，指相反、反对，即事物在运动中会向其自身的对立面转化；其二，指返回、复归，即事物最终返回到原初的状态。这一命题反映了老子及道家对事物运动法则的深刻理解。

The motion of Dao is to transform into the opposite or return to the original state. This concept was proposed by Laozi. Laozi believed that Dao is the fundamental rule of motion and change of things. The essence of this rule is "return," which has two different implications. One indicates the contrary and opposite, namely, a thing in motion may transform into its opposite. The other suggests returning, meaning that a thing eventually returns to its initial state. This concept embodies the profound understanding of Laozi and Daoist scholars about the rule governing the motion of things.

引例 Citation：

◎反者道之动，弱者道之用。(《老子·四十章》)
("道"的运动是向对立面的转化或复归，"道"在起作用时总是柔弱处下的。)

The motion of Dao is transforming into the opposite or returning to the original state; and Dao is soft and humble while it is functioning. (*Laozi*)

fàn'ài 泛爱

Broad Love Extending to All

广泛地爱。在语义学层面，它与"博爱"相同；但在思想史层面，"博爱"通常指爱所有人，而"泛爱"则既指爱所有的人，也指爱一切事物，与孟子

（前372？—前289）的"仁民爱物"、张载（1020—1077）的"民胞物与"异曲同工。

On the semantic level, *fan'ai* (泛爱), like the term *bo'ai* (博爱), means a broad love that extends to all. However, in the history of Chinese thought, it has been used with a different connotation: while *bo'ai* generally suggests "love of all human beings," *fan'ai* infers "love of all humans as well as all things." It means the same as what Mencius (372?-289 BC) advocated that men of virtue should love others and treasure everything on earth, and what Zhang Zai (1020-1077) proposed that all people are brothers and sisters, and all things are companions.

引例 Citations：

◎子曰："弟子入则孝，出则悌，谨而信，泛爱众，而亲仁。"（《论语·学而》）

（孔子说："弟子们在家要孝顺父母，出门要尊重师长，言行要谨慎诚信，广爱众人，亲近有仁德的人。"）

Confucius said, "At home treat parents with reverence, outside treat elders with respect, be circumspect and honest, love all people, and frequent those who are magnanimous and virtuous." (*The Analects*)

◎泛爱万物，天地一体也。（《庄子·天下》）

（广泛地爱一切事物，天地万物是一个有机整体。）

Love all things and creatures, for they form an organic whole. (*Zhuangzi*)

fēimìng 非命

Rejection of Fatalism

反对人事由命运所决定的观念。"非命"是墨家的基本主张之一。墨子（前468？—前376）提出，人民的贫富、国家的治乱都取决于人自身的作为，而不是由命运所决定的。将人事托付于命运，是在推卸行为主体的责任，只会导致国乱民贫。只有依据"兼爱"等道德原则，通过自身的努力作为，才能获得实际的利益。

A belief that events are not predetermined and a denial of fate is a basic component of Mohist thought. Mozi (468?-376 BC) proposed that poverty and turmoil are brought about by our own acts rather than predetermined by fate. Blaming human affairs on fate is nothing other than relieving actors of responsibility for their actions and will only bring chaos to the state and poverty to the people. Only by embracing ethical principles such as impartial love and by our own efforts, can we gain practical benefits.

引例 Citation：

◎执有命者，此天下之厚害也，是故子墨子非也。(《墨子·非命中》)
（主张命运决定人事的人，是天下的大害，因此墨子反对他们的主张。）

Those who hold that there is fate are harmful to the world. For that reason Mozi is opposed to their stand. (*Mozi*)

gé 格

Examine / Study

对人、事、物的考量与推究。是儒家提出的获得正确认识、培养道德良知的途径，具有方法论的意义。"格"亦有规范、准则的意思。用于人物品评，则指人的道德水平和思想境界，即人格。用于文艺批评，主要有三重含义：其一，指诗文写作的基本要求和方法；其二，指作品的品位、品格与境界；其三，指作品的体制、组织结构，是内容特色和形式特征相统一而呈现出的整体格局，仍不离衡量作品水准这一核心意义。

This term means to study or examine things, people or any phenomenon. It is an approach developed by Confucian scholars to help people obtain accurate assessments of things around them and to cultivate morals and ethics, as a kind of methodology. Sometimes the term is used as a noun to refer to a standard or criterion. When the term is used to assess a person's qualifications, it refers to his moral quality which is to say, a person's personality or moral integrity, as well as attainments in learning. In literary criticism, it has three connotations: first of all, it refers to the basic requirements and methods for poem or prose writing; second, it refers to the taste, style, and literary attainment; third, it is about the overall structure of a literary work or how the form and content are integrated. All in all, the term refers to the criteria applied in judging a literary work.

引例 Citations：

◎致知在格物，物格而后知至。(《礼记·大学》)

（获得真知的途径在于推究事实与现象，穷尽事物方方面面的道理，而后才得到真知。)

To study and analyze facts and phenomena is the right approach to obtain knowledge; the truth can only be obtained after facts and phenomena are thoroughly examined and analyzed. (*The Book of Rites*)

◎唐之晚年，诗人无复李、杜豪放之格，然亦务以精意相高。（欧阳修《六一诗话》）

（到了晚唐，诗人们难以再现李杜诗歌那样奔放宏大的境界，但也一定要以构思精巧而一争高下。）

In the late Tang Dynasty, poets no longer possessed the bold, heroic qualities of their predecessors Li Bai and Du Fu. Nonetheless they still competed with each other with regard to the depth of thought and literary refinement. (Ouyang Xiu: *Ouyang Xiu's Criticism of Poetry*)

◎诗之要，有曰格，曰意、曰趣而已。格以辨其体，意以达其情，趣以臻其妙也。（高启《〈独庵集〉序》）

（作诗的关键在于"格"（格局）、"意"（意蕴）和"趣"（趣味）。"格"可以判断其风格体式是否雅正，"意"则是察看其是否表达了真情实感，而"趣"则是衡量其是否达到精妙的境界。）

Structure, content, and appeal are the essentials of poetry. Its structure will reflect the poetic form; its content will convey emotion; and its appeal will determine whether it has achieved a high level of artistry. (Gao Qi: Preface to *Collected Works of Du'an*)

gōngdiào 宫调

Gongdiao (Musical Modes)

中国传统乐学将调式与音高结合，划分、命名音乐类型并描述其特性的基本理论。以宫、商、角、变徵、徵、羽、变宫等七声或其中五声、六声音阶中任何一声为主音，与其他乐音按一定的音程关系（相隔若干音度）组织在一起，均可构成一种调式，其中以宫声为主的调式称"宫"，以其他各声为主者称"调"。七种调式与黄钟、大吕等十二律相配，理论上可配得十二宫七十二调，共为八十四宫调。但在实际音乐中并不全用，如唐宋燕乐只用七宫，每宫四调，共有二十八宫调；南宋词曲音乐用七宫十二调；元代北曲用六宫十一调，南曲用五宫四调；明清以来，最常用者不过五宫四调。有些乐论家对不同宫调所表达的感情特点和适用场合做了规定。宫调理论对于词曲、戏剧、音乐创作具有指导和规范作用，可以运用于古代乐谱翻译，是中国艺术研究的一个重要课题。

Classical Chinese music theory combined tone and pitch to classify and name different types of music, as well as to describe their characteristics. The seven notes are known as *gong* (宫 corresponding to 1 in the numbered musical notation), *shang* (商 corresponding to 2), *jue* (角 corresponding to 3), *bianzhi* (变徵 corresponding to 4), *zhi* (徵 corresponding to 5), *yu* (羽 corresponding to 6) and *biangong* (变宫 corresponding to 7). Any one of them can be used as a major tune along with other notes set in particular intervals to form a mode. The mode with *gong* as the major note is called *gong*, the mode with the rest of the notes as major ones are called *diao*. The seven modes with the accompaniment of 12 temperaments can theoretically have 12 *gongs* and

72 *diaos*, altogether 84 modes of music. However, in practical music, not all the *gongs* and *diaos* were used. Only seven *gongs* with each having four tunes (all together 28 modes of music) were used for imperial court music in the Tang and Song dynasties. Seven *gongs* and 12 *diaos* were used for music to go along with poems in the Southern Song Dynasty. In the Yuan Dynasty, six *gongs* and 11 *diaos* were used for Northern music, and five *gongs* and four *diaos* were used for Southern music. In the Ming and Qing dynasties, only five *gongs* and four *diaos* were often used. Some music critics made rules for different *gongs* and *diaos* to be used for music for different occasions according to their characteristics. The theory of *gongdiao* played a role of direction and regulation in music creation for poems and operas and can be used to translate ancient music. It is an important subject for the study of ancient Chinese art.

引例 Citation：

◎ 凡《大雅》皆宫调曲，《小雅》皆徵调曲，《周》《鲁》二颂皆羽调曲。十五《国风》皆角调曲。周诗三百篇通不用商调，惟《商颂》五篇则皆商调耳。（朱载堉《乐律全书》卷七下）

（《诗经》中凡是《大雅》用的都是宫调的音乐，《小雅》用的都是徵调的音乐，《周颂》和《鲁颂》用的都是羽调的音乐，而十五《国风》用的都是角调的音乐。周代时《诗经》中有三百篇用的都不是商调，只有《商颂》的五篇用的都是商调。）

In *The Book of Songs*, "Major Court Hymns" are all in the *gong* mode, "Minor Court Hymns" all in the *zhi* mode, "Eulogies of Zhou" and "Eulogies of Lu" in the *yu* mode, and "Ballads" from the fifteen states all in the *jue* mode. Of all the works in *The Book of Songs* in the Zhou Dynasty, only "Eulogies of Shang," altogether five pieces, use the *shang* mode. (Zhu Zaiyu: *A Collection of Writings on Music and Calendar*)

gōngzhèng 公正

Fair / Just

公平正义或公平正直。"公"与"厶（私）"相反，无偏私，不以个人为中心考虑问题；"正"与"曲"相反，有两层含义：其一，有以正义为基础的共同的准则。其二，能以此端正自己与他人的一切行为，不偏斜，不枉曲。"公正"主要体现为国家、社会有共同的道义和规范，所有人都能以此约束自己并对他人行为正确与否作出判断。在现代社会，公正主要体现在制度公正、法律公正、社会财富与公共资源分配公正及人心公正等方面，被认为是培育美好品德、构建美好社会的核心价值之一。

The expression means fair and just. *Gong* (公), the opposite of *si* (私 private), means impartial and not self-centered. *Zheng* (正), the opposite of *qu* (曲 crooked), has two meanings. One is shared norms based on justice, and the other is making oneself comply with these norms in one's behavior and stay unbiased and impartial in one's relationship with others. Fairness is expressed mainly in a state or society having a common morality and norms with which all people are bound and which people use to judge whether others are doing right. In modern society, fairness finds its expression mainly in the way that institutions, laws, and people are just and social wealth and public resources are fairly distributed. It is seen as one of the core values conducive to good morality and society.

引例 Citations：

◎毋以私好恶害公正，察民所恶，以自为戒。(《管子·桓公问》)

（不要以自己的喜欢或不喜欢损害公平正义，要知道百姓所厌恶的做法并以之为戒。）

Do not harm the fairness because of personal likes and dislikes. Find out what the people detest and take that as a warning to oneself. (*Guanzi*)

◎太宗曰："古称至公者，盖谓平恕无私。"（吴兢《贞观政要·公平》）

（唐太宗说："古代讲的最公正，大概是说持心公平宽恕、绝无偏私。"）

Emperor Taizong of the Tang Dynasty said, "What the ancient people described as the greatest fairness probably means impartiality and forbearance without any self-interest." (Wu Jing: *Important Political Affairs of the Zhenguan Reign*)

◎天下所以平者，政平也；政所以平者，人平也；人所以平者，心平也。（《艺文类聚》卷二十二引）

（天下所以能做到公平，只因有国家政事的公平；国家政事所以做到公平，只因掌管政事的人公平；掌管政事的人所以做到公平，只因他们的内心有公平。）

All under heaven enjoys fairness when its governance is fair. Governance is fair when the men who govern are fair. The men are fair when their minds are fair. (*An Anthology of Pre-Tang Dynasty Literature*)

gǔwén yùndòng 古文运动

Classical Prose Movement

指唐代中期至北宋时期提倡用古文创作的文学革新运动。其特点是反对六朝以来的骈文创作，兼有思想运动和社会运动的性质。这一运动的代表者，有唐代的韩愈（768—824）、柳宗元（773—819），以及宋代的欧阳修（1007—1072）、苏洵（1009—1066）、王安石（1021—1086）、曾巩（1019—1083）、苏轼（1037—1101）、苏辙（1039—1112）等人。"古文"相对于"骈文"而言，这一概念由韩愈最先提出，指先秦两汉的散文，其特点是句式长短不限，不追求声律和对偶，在内容上注重表达思想、反映现实生活。"骈文"指六朝以来讲究排偶、辞藻、声律、典故的文体。骈文中虽有优秀作品，但大多形式僵化、内容空虚。韩愈倡导继承两汉的文学传统，文以明道，得到了柳宗元等人的大力支持并形成声势浩大的"古文运动"。韩愈提倡古文的实质是将改革文风与复兴儒学道统结合起来，把文章写作引向为政教服务。但骈文并未就此绝迹，晚唐以后还在流行。北宋欧阳修凭借其政治地位，大力提倡古文，他的同辈苏洵，学生王安石、曾巩、苏轼、苏辙，苏轼门下又有黄庭坚（1045—1105）、陈师道（1053—1102）、张耒（1054—1114）、秦观（1049—1100）、晁补之（1053—1110）等人，都是古文能手，各树旗帜，最终使宋代古文运动达到波澜壮阔的地步。

It refers to the literary reform movement in the mid-Tang to the Northern Song period. It opposed rigidly rhythmical prose featuring parallelism and excessive elegance that had been popular in the Six Dynasties, and advocated a return to writing in "truly" classical Chinese. This movement was both intellectual and social in nature. Its representative figures included Han Yu (768-824) and Liu Zongyuan (773-819) of the Tang Dynasty and Ouyang Xiu (1007-1072), Su Xun (1009-1066), Wang Anshi (1021-1086), Zeng Gong (1019-1083), Su Shi (1037-1101), and Su Zhe (1039-1112) of the Song Dynasty. In this particular context, the notion of classical prose stood in contrast to rigidly rhythmical prose. Classical prose, first proposed by Han Yu, referred to the prose of the Qin, Western Han, and Eastern Han dynasties. It featured poetic lines of flexible lengths with no particular regard for metric pattern and parallel structure. In terms of content, classical prose aimed to express ideas and reflect real life. Rigidly rhythmical prose, on the other hand, was a style of writing popular in the pre-Tang period which had rigid requirement about the use of parallelism, elegant wording, prosody, melody, and allusions. Although there were good works in this genre, most were rigid in form and hollow in content. In view of this, Han Yu called for a return to the literary tradition of the Western and Eastern Han dynasties to reform literary writing. He gained the strong support of eminent men of letters such as Liu Zongyuan. Together, they launched what was later widely known as the Classical Prose Movement. Han Yu took this initiative to combine the reform of literary writing with the revival of Confucian moralism so as to enable literary writing to promote better governance. But rhythmical prose did not die out altogether; it continued into the late Tang period. Northern Song writer Ouyang Xiu, with strong political influence, championed the revival of classical prose. His contemporary Su Xun, as well as his students Wang Anshi, Zeng Gong, Su Shi, and Su Zhe all wrote classical prose with distinctive styles. Influenced by Su Shi, Huang Tingjian (1045-1105), Chen Shidao (1053-1102), Zhang Lei (1054-1114), Qin Guan (1049-1100), and Chao Buzhi (1053-1110) also became prominent prose writers. Thanks to the efforts of these literary figures, the Classical Prose Movement flourished in the Song Dynasty.

引例 Citations：

◎时时应事作俗下文字，下笔令人惭。……不知古文，真何用于今世也，然以俟知者知耳。(韩愈《与冯宿论文书》)
(我经常为应付世事而写平庸的应酬文章，下笔时令人惭愧。……不知古文对今世真的有什么用啊，那么还是等待懂的人赏识吧。)

So often, I have to write just for the purpose of socializing. This makes me feel ashamed… What good can classical prose do for today's world? I just hope that there will be people who can truly appreciate our writing. (Han Yu: Letter to Feng Su on Prose Writing)

◎苏子瞻曰:"子美之诗,退之之文,鲁公之书,皆集大成者也。"(陈师道《后山诗话》引)

(苏轼说过:"杜甫的诗、韩愈的文章、颜真卿的书法,都是集合了各家的优点而达到最高成就的。")

Su Shi said, "Du Fu's poems, Han Yu's prose, and Yan Zhenqing's calligraphy, by drawing on all that is best in great poets, prose writers, and calligraphers, have reached the highest level of artistic attainment." (Chen Shidao: *Houshan's Understanding of Poetry*)

hánxù 含蓄

Subtle Suggestion

　　文艺作品的一种创作技巧与风格,用简约的语言和浅近的艺术形象委婉表达出丰富深远的情感意蕴,使欣赏者能从中获得回味无穷的美感。中国古代的文学艺术作品中既有直率真实的表现方式,亦有含蓄蕴藉的表达手法。含蓄这一术语源于诗歌的讽谏传统及道家思想,主张作品的情感、意蕴应当内敛,外在形象的描写要借助充实的内在意蕴而感染读者,形成言近旨远、意在言外的审美效果。唐代司空图(837—908)将其列为二十四种诗歌风格之一。含蓄是作家修养、创作技巧与文学作品的风格和境界的高度统一。

A technique or style in creating literary works, it refers to the use of concise language in portraying a simple artistic image, whose rich feelings and implications are elicited in a subtle manner, so that readers can intuit multiple hidden meanings. One finds a straightforward and factual manner of expression in early literary and artistic works in China, as well as the subtle mode of expression. Because this technique originally evolved from Daoist thought and, in the early period, was employed as a means of criticizing powerful individuals in poetry, it stresses the expression of emotion in a subtly suggestive manner, such that the depiction of images should be supported by a rich undertone or hidden meaning that can appeal to readers. The language should be simple and plain but still leave sufficient room for readers to seize upon hidden meanings. Sikong Tu (837-908), a literary critic in the Tang Dynasty, listed it as one of the twenty-four styles of poetry writing. Subtle suggestion imparts a high degree of unity to a writer's cultural attainments, creative technique, as well as his literary style and imagery.

引例 Citations：

◎不著一字，尽得风流。语不涉己，若不堪忧。是有真宰，与之沉浮。（司空图《二十四诗品·含蓄》）
（虽然没有写上一字，却尽得其意蕴之美妙。文辞虽没有直接抒写自己的忧伤，读时却使人好像忧伤不已。这是因为事物有着真实自然的情理，在与作品一起或沉或浮。）

Without penning down a word about it, yet it is overfilled with what it intends to express. Without mentioning the writer's own sorrow, yet one can feel it there. It is because the genuine and natural feelings reside there, that one's mood rises and falls with the work that conveys them. (Sikong Tu: Twenty-four Styles of Poetry)

◎语贵含蓄。东坡云："言有尽而意无穷者，天下之至言也。"（姜夔《白石道人诗说》）

（语言表达以含蓄为贵。苏东坡说："用有限的文辞表达无穷的意义，这是天下公认的至理名言啊。"）

The merit of expressing oneself lies in presenting one's opinions with subtlety. Su Dongpo once said, "There is a limit to the words one can use in writing a poem, but there is no limit to the meaning a poem may deliver. This is universally acknowledged." (Jiang Kui: *The Poetry Theory of Baishi Daoren*)

◎含蓄无穷，词之要诀。含蓄者，意不浅露，语不穷尽，句中有余味，篇中有余意，其妙不外寄言而已。（沈祥龙《论词随笔》）

（有着无限的蕴含是作词的要诀。含蓄就是意蕴不要简单肤浅，用词不要将意蕴全都说完，句子要给人留有回味的余地，整部作品有让人进一步思考的空间，其精妙之处不外就是在有限的词句上寄寓无限的意蕴而已。）

The key to writing great *ci* lyrics is the subtle suggestion of limitless meaning. Subtle suggestion means that the meaning is never simply obvious, yet the words will forever echo in one's mind. A line should leave enough room for further thought, and a poem enough meaning for readers to ponder. The beauty of this method lies in expressing unlimited subtle meaning in simple language. (Shen Xianglong: *Essays on Ci Poetry*)

hányǒng 涵泳

Be Totally Absorbed (in Reading and Learning)

原指阅读经典作品时，要像潜泳一样沉浸其中、反复玩味，方能有所收获，激发自己的情志和感悟。作为一种读书做学问的方法，它强调调动自己的经验和学养，努力思考书中的问题、观点、材料及事实，使自己的学问如源头活水而常新。作为一种理解与诠释文艺作品的方法，它强调努力进入作品特定的情境，通过反复体会与咀嚼，最终领略作品的深层意蕴及审美意境。它也表明文艺作品具有兴发志意和感化人心的效力。

This term originally refers to an attitude in reading classics, requiring one to become deeply absorbed in the work as if one were submerged in water, repeatedly ruminating on its meaning until one is able to fully digest its significance so that it informs one's own feelings and insights. In time this becomes a way of learning, impelling one to mobilize one's own experience and accumulated knowledge to think deeply about what he is reading so that knowledge is endlessly renewed and refreshed. As a method of understanding and interpreting literary works, it requires one to place one's own thought in the particular world of the work so that one becomes deeply aware of why the work was so written and can master its subtle meanings and aesthetic conception. This method is premised on the understanding that literary works can be deeply inspiring and enlightening.

引例 Citations：

◎学者读书，须要敛身正坐，缓视微吟，虚心涵泳，切己省察。(《朱子语类》卷十一)

（学者读书，必须收腹端坐，慢慢看，轻声念，放空心灵，沉浸其中，并结合自身经验进行思考和体察。）

When a scholar reads a book, he must sit straight, read attentively, read out softly, focus all his thought on the book, be entirely absorbed in it, and meditate on its significance from his own experience. (*Categorized Conversations of Master Zhu Xi*)

◎此等语言自有个血脉流通处，但涵泳久之，自然见得条畅浃洽，不必多引外来道理、言语，却壅滞却诗人活底意思也。（朱熹《答何叔京》）
（这些语言都有内在的血脉连通之处，只要沉潜其中反复玩味，自然能够理清头绪，融会贯通，不必引用很多外来的道理和言论，这样反而遮蔽诗人真正想要表达的意思。）

Such language has an inner coherence and logical line of thought. When a person has been deeply absorbed in it for long, he naturally understands how to articulate its complexities and unite its core ideas. There is no need to rely on theories and discussions extraneous to the work. To do so would only be to stifle what the poet intended to express. (Zhu Xi: In Response to He Shujing)

◎熟绎上下文，涵泳以求其立言之指，则差别毕见（xiàn）矣。（王夫之《姜斋诗话》卷二）
（细致推究上下文的联系，沉浸其中以求把握文章的主旨，那么不同文章的差别就会完全显现出来了。）

By carefully studying the literary context of a text, and by becoming so absorbed in the text as to master its essence, one will be able to discern the essential differences between different literary works. (Wang Fuzhi: *Desultory Remarks on Poetry from Ginger Studio*)

hànyuèfǔ 汉乐府

Yuefu Poetry

指汉代的乐府诗。"乐府"本是秦以后由朝廷设立的用来训练乐工、采集民歌并配器作曲的专门官署，后转指由乐府机关所采集、配乐并由乐工演唱的民歌。乐府诗是继《诗经》之后古代民歌的一次创造，是与"诗经""楚辞"并列的诗歌形态。至今保存的汉乐府民歌有五六十首，大都真实反映了当时社会生活的各个方面，表现出纯真质朴的思想感情，并由此形成反映普通民众声音与情感的文学创作传统。其中最有特色与成就的是描写女性生活的作品。汉代以后将可以入乐的诗歌及仿乐府古题而写的诗歌统称为乐府。

Yuefu (乐府) poems were written in the Han Dynasty. Originally, *yuefu* was a government office set up by the imperial court to train musicians, collect folk songs and ballads, compose music, and match musical instruments to it. It later came to refer to folk songs and ballads collected, matched with music, and played by court musicians. Poems of this style represented a new creation of ancient folk songs and ballads in the years after *The Book of Songs* was compiled, and equaled *The Book of Songs* and *Odes of Chu* in importance. About 50 to 60 *yuefu* poems have been handed down to this day. They truthfully depicted various aspects of society at the time and revealed genuine emotions, thus creating a literary tradition reflecting ordinary people's sentiments. In particular, *yuefu* poems were noted for their vivid depiction of women's life. All poems that could be chanted or were written with *yuefu* themes were collectively called *yuefu* poems in later times.

引例 Citations：

◎自孝武立乐府而采歌谣，于是有代、赵之讴，秦、楚之风。皆感于哀乐，缘事而发……（《汉书·艺文志》）

（自从汉武帝设立乐府并采集歌谣，这之后就有了代、赵之地的吟唱及秦、楚等地的民歌。它们都是受内心悲喜情绪的影响或者受到某件事情的触发而产生的……）

After Emperor Wu of the Han Dynasty set up an office to collect folk songs and ballads, folk songs from the Dai and Zhao regions, and ballads from the Qin and Chu regions could be heard. They were all created to express people's joy and sorrow or were inspired by certain events… (*The History of the Han Dynasty*)

◎乐府者,"声依永,律和声"也。(刘勰《文心雕龙·乐府》)
(乐府诗,就是"随诗的吟唱而有抑扬疾徐的声音变化,再用音律调和声音"。)

Yuefu poems vary in rhythm and tone and are accompanied by music when chanted. (Liu Xie: *The Literary Mind and the Carving of Dragons*)

háofàngpài 豪放派

The *Haofang* School / The Bold and Unconstrained School

宋词两大流派之一。内容多写家国大事、人生情怀,其特点是境界壮阔宏大,气象豪迈雄放,常常运用诗文创作手法及典故,而且不拘音律。最先用"豪放"评词的是苏轼(1037—1101),南宋人已明确将苏轼、辛弃疾(1140—1207)作为豪放词的代表。北宋范仲淹(989—1052)《渔家傲》词开豪放之先,经苏轼大力创作"壮词"而成一派词风。中原沦陷后,南宋政权偏安江南,不以收复失地为意,许多词人报国无望,因而逐渐形成慷慨悲壮的词风,产生了豪放派领袖辛弃疾及陈与义(1090—1139)、叶梦得(1077—1148)、朱敦儒(1081—1159)、张元干(1091—1170?)、张孝祥(1132—1170)、陆游(1125—1210)、陈亮(1143—1194)、刘过(1154—1206)等一大批杰出词人。他们抒发报国情怀,将个体的命运与家国命运紧密联系在一起,进一步拓宽了词的表现领域,丰富了词的表现手法，大大提升了词在文学史上的地位。豪放派词人虽以豪放为主体风格，却也不乏清秀婉约之作，故不可一概而论。有些词作出现议论和用典过多、音律不精或过于散文化，也是毋庸讳言的。

This is one of the two *ci* (词) lyric schools of the Song Dynasty, which mainly dealt with major affairs of the nation and expresses noble aspirations. It featured broad vision and bold expression, often employing the methods of prose poetry and uninhibited by metric stereotypes. The first poet who used the term "bold and unconstrained" was Su Shi (1037-1101) who, together with Xin Qiji (1140-1207), was widely acclaimed by Southern Song critics as the leading poets of this school. The Northern Song writer Fan Zhongyan (989-1052) created this school with his *ci* lyric, A Fisherman's Song, which grew into a major poetic style thanks mainly to Su Shi's contribution. After the Central Plains fell to the Jin forces, the Song court fled south of the Yangtze River and was too weak to recover the lost territory. Many *ci* poets, led by Xin Qiji and supported by other prominent poets such as Chen Yuyi (1090-1139), Ye Mengde (1077-1148), Zhu Dunru (1081-1159), Zhang Yuangan (1091-1170?), Zhang Xiaoxiang (1132-1170), Lu You (1125-1210), Chen Liang (1143-1194), and Liu Guo (1154-1206), expressed their longing to return to the north in verses of a stirring style. They voiced their patriotic sentiments and identified their own fate with that of the whole nation. They thus enriched *ci* lyrics' ways of expression and greatly lifted its status in the history of literature. Although poets of this school wrote in the bold and unconstrained style, they occasionally wrote graceful and subtle *ci* poems. And some of their works contained too many commentaries and allusions, were careless about the use of metric schemes, and read more like prose than poetry.

引例 Citations：

◎词体大略有二：一体婉约，一体豪放。婉约者欲其辞情蕴藉，豪放者欲其气象恢弘。盖亦存乎其人，如秦少游之作多是婉约，苏子瞻之作多是豪放。大约词体以婉约为正。（张綖（yán）《诗余图谱·凡例》）

（词的风格大约有两种，一种是婉约，一种是豪放。婉约风格的词，其词句和情感追求含蓄之美，豪放词则追求气魄宏大。大概是由于作者的气质所致，如秦观的作品多是婉约之作，而苏轼的作品多是豪放之作。大致说来，词的风格以婉约为正宗。）

Ci lyrics can be divided into two types: the graceful and restrained vs. the bold and unconstrained. The first type of poems features subtle expression of one's feelings, whereas the second type is far more explicit and has a broader vision. This distinction is due to different dispositions of poets. Qin Guan's *ci* lyrics are mostly graceful and subtle, whereas Su Shi's tend to be bold and exuberant. Generally, the graceful and restrained style follows more closely the original spirit of *ci* lyrics than the bold and unconstrained style. (Zhang Yan: *The Metric Schemes of Ci Lyrics*)

◎张南湖论词派有二：一曰婉约，一曰豪放。仆谓婉约以易安为宗，豪放惟幼安称首，皆吾济南人，难乎为继矣！（王士禛《花草蒙拾》）

（张綖论词派有二：一是婉约派，一是豪放派。我认为婉约派以李清照为第一，豪放派以辛弃疾为第一，他们都是我们济南人，之后就后继无人了。）

According to Zhang Yan, *ci* lyrics can either be graceful and restrained or bold and unconstrained. I believe that Li Qingzhao is the best of the former and Xin Qiji the best of the latter. They were both natives of Ji'nan. After them, no great *ci* poet has emerged in our province. (Wang Shizhen: *Random Notes on Ci Poetry*)

hào zhàn bì wáng, wàng zhàn bì wēi 好战必亡，忘战必危

Those Who Like to Go to War Will Perish; Those Who Forget War Will Be in Danger.

热衷于战争必然灭亡，而忘记战争必然危险。亦即是说，好战的国家必然导致自身灭亡，而没有战备的国家又会使自己处于危险境地。"好战"是指为了自身利益，不顾道义，热衷于对外挑起冲突和战争；"忘战"是指忘记战争可能降临到自己头上，不做相应准备。古人认为，应该本着仁爱精神处理国内、国际事务；战争会使国力消耗，生灵涂炭，即便是为了保国安民而"以战止战"的正义战争，也是不得已而采取的行动。这句话，既表明了战争与国家兴衰的辩证法，也彰显了中华民族爱好和平的"文"的精神。

Those who are warmongering will inevitably be destroyed, and those who forget war will inevitably land in danger. That is, countries that like to make war are certain to bring destruction upon themselves, and countries which are not prepared for war will find themselves in dangerous situations. *Haozhan* (好战) refers to those who are keen to stir up conflicts and wars externally for their own interests and in disregard of moral principles; *wangzhan* (忘战) is to forget that war may befall oneself and thus fail to be appropriately prepared for it. Ancient Chinese believed that domestic and international affairs should be handled with a spirit of loving others. Wars exhaust a country's resources and lead to loss of life; even a just war, a "war to end wars" conducted to defend a country and safeguard its people, should be a last resort. This phrase both illustrates the dialectical relationship between war and the rise and fall of countries and demonstrates the "civil" nature of the Chinese people who love peace.

引例 Citations：

◎故国虽大，好战必亡；天下虽安，忘战必危。天下既平，天下大恺，春蒐（sōu）秋狝（xiǎn），诸侯春振旅，秋治兵，所以不忘战也。(《司马法·仁本》)

（所以，国家虽然强大，但如果热衷于战争，必然会灭亡；天下虽然安宁，但如果忘记战争危险的存在，必然会使自己处于危险境地。即使天下已经太平，百姓生活安乐，每年春秋两季天子还是要用打猎进行军事演习，各诸侯国也要在春秋整顿军队和进行军事训练，这都是为了不忘战争的存在。）

Therefore though a country be powerful, if it is fond of war it will surely perish; though the land be at peace, those who forget war will inevitably be in danger. Hence even when there is peace throughout the land and the people lead settled lives, hunting is conducted in the spring and fall as military exercises. The vassal states train their troops and hold military drills in the spring and fall so that they do not forget war. (*The General Commander's Treatise on War*)

◎夫怒者逆德也，兵者凶器也，争者末节也。夫务战胜、穷武事者，未有不悔者也。(《资治通鉴·汉纪十·孝武皇帝元朔元年》)

（愤怒违逆德义，用兵带来灾祸，争斗则是最不值得做的事情。那些追求赢得战争、穷兵黩武的人，没有不后悔的。）

To be angered is contrary to virtue, to wage war is an invitation of disaster, and fighting is the most unworthy action. Warmongers who seek victories in war always end in regret. (*History as a Mirror*)

héwéiguì 和为贵

Harmony Is Most Precious.

以和谐为贵。"和"，和谐、恰当，是在尊重事物差异性、多样性基础上的和谐共存。本指"礼"的作用就是使不同等级的人既保持一定差别又彼此和谐共存，各得其所，各安其位，相得益彰，从而实现全社会的"和而不同"，为儒家处理人际关系的重要伦理原则。后泛指人与人之间、团体与团体之间、国家与国家之间和谐、和睦、和平、融洽的关系状态。它体现了中华民族反对暴力冲突、崇尚和平与和谐的"文"的精神。

Make harmony a top priority. *He* (和) indicates congruity and appropriateness. It is a state of congenial co-existence on the basis of due respect for differences and diversity. At first, this phrase referred to the role of *li* (礼 rites / social norms) which is to keep citizens of distinct social status co-existing in a harmonious way, with everybody having his or her own place and staying there contentedly for mutual benefits, resulting in a "harmonious yet diverse" society. It is an important moral concept of the Confucian school in managing inter-personal relations. The term later evolved to refer in general to harmonious, congenial, peaceful, and agreeable relationships among people, groups, and states. It epitomizes the "civil" nature of the Chinese people, who oppose violent conflicts and aspire for peace and harmony.

引例 Citation：

◎有子曰："礼之用，和为贵。先王之道，斯为美，小大由之。有所不行，知和而和，不以礼节之，亦不可行也。"（《论语·学而》）

（有子说："礼的应用，以和谐为贵。古代君主的治国方法，可宝贵的地方就在这里，不论大事小事都依照"和"的原则去做。也有行不通的时候，如果仍一味为了和谐而和谐，而不用礼来加以节制，也是不可行的。"）

Youzi said, "Make harmony a top priority in the application of rites. That is a key feature that characterizes governance by sovereign rulers in ancient past. Always act upon the rule of harmony, no matter whether the issue at hand is minor or major. Sometimes, however, this rule may fail to work. If one insists on seeking harmony just for the sake of harmony instead of qualifying it with rites, then there will be no hope to succeed." (*The Analects*)

huānghán 荒寒

Grim and Desolate

古代诗词绘画作品中所描写的荒僻凄寒的环境及所体现出的孤寂凄冷的心境。唐宋时期一些远戍边关或遭贬谪的诗人，因仕途失意或不为时人理解而倍感环境的荒凉和内心的孤独，在诗歌作品中常常营造一种荒僻凄寒的氛围或意境，以此传达自己百折不回、独善其身的心志，使之成为一种独特的审美追求和超越现实的审美方式。追求荒寒意境的绘画则更充满一种独与天地往来的精神和与自然融为一体的情趣。这类诗画代表着中国文化的一种独特品位与风格。

This term refers to desolate and barren landscapes described or portrayed in classical poems or paintings that convey a feeling of loneliness and desolation. During the Tang and Song dynasties, some poets who were either exiled or sent to work at border garrisons did not only dwell in desolate places but also felt the dire bleakness within as they saw no hope for their future and they were being unappreciated and unrecognized for what they were worth. As a result, in their poetry they would create bleak, desolate scenes with a view to expressing their perseverance and determination to maintain personal integrity. In doing so they created a unique artistic method capable of transcending reality. Paintings depicting grim, desolate scenes suggest the lonely communication of man with nature, expressing as well the integration of man with nature. Such poems and paintings represent a kind of taste and style characteristic of Chinese culture.

引例 Citations：

◎尤工写塞外荒寒之景，殆扈从时所身历，故言这亲切如此。其慢词则凡近拖沓，远不如其小令，岂词才所限欤？（蔡嵩云《柯亭词论》）

（[纳兰性德的词]尤其长于写塞外荒寒的景象，应该是在随皇帝出巡时的亲身经历，因此他的描写才如此亲切。而他较长的词作则近乎拖沓，远远不如他的小令，难道是他作词的才力所限的缘故吗？）

The vivid portrayals of grim and desolate scenes beyond the Great Wall in Nalan Xingde's *ci* poems derive from his personal experience escorting the emperor on inspection tours, so that his portrayals are so close to nature. On the other hand his long *ci* poems are a bit loose, not as good as his short ones. Is it because his talent had its limits? (Cai Songyun: *Keting's Comments on Ci Poetry*)

◎雪图自摩诘以后，惟称营丘、华原、河阳、道宁（nìng）。然古劲有余，而荒寒不逮。（恽格《南田画跋·题石谷雪图》）

（画雪景的作品自王维之后，可以称道的是李成、范宽、李唐、许道宁。然而他们的画作古朴苍劲有余，但荒寒意境上却不及王维的作品。）

As for snowy scenes produced after the time of Wang Wei, those worth notice were by Li Cheng, Fan Kuan, Li Tang, and Xu Daoning. Although their brushwork was amply vigorous, they could not compare with Wang Wei in regards to that sense of grim desolation. (Yun Ge: *Nantian's Comments on Paintings*)

Huáng Hé 黄河

The Yellow River

中国第二大河，发源于青藏高原，自西向东流经青海、四川、甘肃、宁夏、内蒙古、陕西、山西、河南、山东9个省（自治区），注入渤海，全长约5464公里，为世界著名大河。因多泥沙色黄而得名，是中华民族的摇篮和中国古代文化的重要发源地，被称为中国人的"母亲河"。她不仅是一条自然河流，而且已经成为中国人重要的文化意象和文化符号，象征中华民族自强不息、百折不挠、勇往直前的精神品格。

Originating in the Qinghai-Tibet Plateau, the Yellow River is the second longest waterway in China, flowing eastward through the provinces of Qinghai, Sichuan, Gansu, the Ningxia Hui Autonomous Region, and the Inner Mongolia Autonomous Region, as well as the provinces of Shaanxi, Shanxi, Henan, and Shandong before emptying into the Bohai Sea. With a total length of 5,464 kilometers, the Yellow River is one of the major waterways in the world. The river is so named because of its yellowish color caused by the large amount of silts washed into it. Considered the cradle of the Chinese nation and Chinese culture, the river is therefore known as the Mother River among the Chinese, and has become an important cultural image and sign for the Chinese nation. It symbolizes the heroism and perseverance with which the Chinese nation forges ahead against all odds.

引例 Citation：

◎白日依山尽，黄河入海流。欲穷千里目，更上一层楼。（王之涣《登鹳雀楼》）

（太阳依傍着西边的大山落下，黄河向着东方的大海奔流。要想眺望千里远，必须再上一层楼。）

The setting sun beyond the mountains glows, the Yellow River seaward flows. Going to the top of the pavilion, and you will have a panoramic river view reaching the horizon. (Wang Zhihuan: Climbing the Guanque Tower)

huìmín 惠民

Benefit the People

惠爱民众，施惠于民。"惠民"属于"仁政"，是"爱民"理念的具体体现，重在把财富分给百姓，给百姓好处。它所强调的是，治国者及各级官员要得到百姓的拥护，就必须把百姓的实际利益放在第一位。亦即说，各项政策、措施必须代表、保障、实现百姓的实际利益，必须藏富于民，不能与民争利，更不能巧取豪夺。

The term means to benefit and provide for the people. *Huimin* (惠民) is a concrete manifestation of benevolent governance and loving the people, with focus on dividing wealth among the people and benefiting them. The emphasis is on placing the interests of the people first, so that they will support both ruler and government officials. Specifically this means all policies and measures must be in the public interest, must fulfill and ensure the real needs of the people, and keep wealth with them; they should not conflict with the public interest, or worse, be deceitful or resort to force.

引例 Citations：

◎惟天惠民，惟辟奉天。（《尚书·泰誓中》）

（上天是惠爱民众的，君主应当遵奉上天旨意［惠爱民众］。）

Heaven benefits the people, and a ruler should follow the will of heaven. (*The Book of History*)

◎分人以财谓之惠。（《孟子·滕文公上》）

（把财物分给众人就叫做"惠"。）

Dividing wealth among the people is called *hui*, or benefiting the people. (*Mencius*)

◎景公问政于师旷曰："太师将奚以教寡人？"师旷曰："君必惠民而已。"……反国，发禀粟以赋众贫，散府余财以赐孤寡，仓无陈粟，府无余财，宫妇不御者出嫁之，七十受禄米。（《韩非子·外储说右上》）

（齐景公［在晋国］向师旷请教如何处理政事，说："您有何指教？"师旷说："您只是要一定施惠于民罢了。"……［齐景公］回到齐国后，打开粮仓将粮食分给贫困的民众，打开府库将多余的钱财赐给孤寡之人，粮仓里没有陈年的粮食，府库也没有多余的钱财，没有临幸过的宫女都嫁了出去，七十岁以上的人可得到国家供给的粮食。）

When Duke Jing of Qi was in the State of Jin, he asked Shi Kuang about how to rule, saying, "What is your advice?" Shi Kuang answered, "All you need to do is look after your people." …The duke returned to the State of Qi, opened the state granaries, and divided up the grain among the poor; he opened the palace treasury and distributed money to those without family to support them. There was no more grain from previous years or unused wealth. Palace maids who had not found favor with him were allowed to leave and marry, and people over seventy were provided with grain by the state. (*Hanfeizi*)

jī 几

Ji (Omen)

事物产生或变化的征兆。古人认为，新事物产生或旧事物发生变化，以及人心善恶的分化之前，都会出现微小的征兆，也即是"几"。"几"或显现于外，或隐藏于旧事物的内部。人应培养发现、把握几兆的能力。只有善于发现事物出现或变化的几兆，并适时加以利用，才能够预见、把握事物发展变化的方向，以实现趋利避害。

Ji (几) refers to an omen indicating the emerging or changing of things. Ancient Chinese believed that a subtle omen would appear before something new emerged or when something old was about to change, or before the differentiation of good and evil in human nature occurred. An omen is either visible or hidden inside something old. One should develop the ability to identify and use an omen. When one is adept at identifying an omen that something is emerging or changing and makes use of it at the appropriate moment, one can foresee and grasp the way things emerge and change, thus pursuing the desired course and avoiding harm.

引例 Citations：

◎几者，动之微，吉凶之先见者也。君子见几而作，不俟终日。(《周易·系辞下》)

("几"是事物变化的微小征兆，预示着吉凶的结果。君子发现几兆就适时行动，不需要长时间等待。)

Ji means a subtle omen of change predicting good or evil. A man of virtue acts at the right moment without hesitation when he sees an omen. (*The Book of Changes*)

◎ 几者，动之微，善恶之所由分也。（朱熹《通书注》）

("几"是事物变化的微小征兆，人心的善恶也由此分化。)

Ji means a subtle omen of change in things, and it indicates the differentiation of good and evil in human nature. (Zhu Xi: *Annotations on The Gist of Confucian Thought*)

jǐsuǒbùyù, wùshīyúrén 己所不欲，勿施于人

Do Not Do to Others What You Do Not Want Others to Do to You.

自己不愿意的，不要强加给别人。这是孔子（前551—前479）所提倡的"恕道"（推己及人的原则），以自己的心意推测、理解别人的心意，亦即今之所谓设身处地，换位思考。其哲学基础是"性相近"（人的本性是相近的）。它是儒家处理人与人关系的重要原则，如今也被引申为反对强权政治的国际关系原则，其基本精神是仁爱、平等与宽容。

Do not impose on others what you do not want yourself. That is the "way of being considerate" advocated by Confucius (551-479 BC). It calls for using one's own mind to infer and understand other people's minds. In today's words, it means to put oneself into others' shoes or to think from their positions. Its philosophical basis lies in the similarity of people's basic natures.

It is an important principle put forth by Confucians to govern inter-personal relationships, and is now extended to international relationship management to counter power politics. Its essential elements are benevolence, equality, and tolerance.

引例 Citations：

◎子曰："性相近也，习相远也。"(《论语·阳货》)

（孔子说："人的本性是相近的，由于环境的习染才有了差别。"）

Confucius said, "Human nature is similar at birth, only made different by the environment." (*The Analects*)

◎子贡问曰："有一言而可以终身行之者乎？"子曰："其恕乎！己所不欲，勿施于人。"(《论语·卫灵公》)

（子贡问道："有没有一句教导可以让我终身奉行呢？"孔子说："那就是恕吧！自己不想要的，不要施加于他人。"）

Zigong asked, "Is there any teaching that can serve as a lasting principle for conduct in one's whole life?" Confucius replied, "Surely that is to be considerate! Do not do to others what you do not want others to do to you." (*The Analects*)

Jiàn'ān fēnggǔ 建安风骨

The Jian'an Literary Style

又称"汉魏风骨"。指汉献帝建安年间（196—220）至魏初这一时期的文学作品中由刚健悲慨的思想感情与清朗遒劲的文辞凝结而成的时代精神和总体风格。汉末政治动荡，战乱频繁，人民流离失所。这一时期的代表作家曹操（155—220）、曹丕（187—226）、曹植（192—232）、孔融（153—208）、陈琳（？—217）、王粲（177—217）、徐干（171—218）、阮瑀（165？—212）、应玚（？—217）、刘桢（？—217）和女诗人蔡琰等人，继承了汉乐府民歌的现实主义传统，在创作中多直面社会动乱，反映民生疾苦及个人怀抱，抒发了建功立业的理想和积极进取的精神，表现出刚健、向上的抱负和豪迈、悲慨的情怀。"建安文学"的总体风格是悲凉慷慨、风骨遒劲、华美壮阔，具有鲜明的时代特征和个性特征，形成了文学史上独特的"建安风骨"，从而被后人尊为典范，其中又以诗歌成就最为突出。

The Jian'an literary style, also known as the Han–Wei literary style, refers to the literary style from the Jian'an era (196–220) of the Han Dynasty to the early Wei Kingdom, featuring powerful expression of passion, anxiety, and indignation. The final years of the Han Dynasty saw political turmoil, incessant wars, and displacement of people. Leading literary figures like Cao Cao (155-220), Cao Pi (187-226), and Cao Zhi (192-232), Kong Rong (153-208), Chen Lin (?-217), Wang Can (177-217), Xu Gan (171-218), Ruan Yu (165?-212), Ying Yang (?-217), and Liu Zhen (?-217), as well as female poet Cai Yan, inherited the realistic tradition of the folksongs of the Han Dynasty. In their writings, they dealt with subjects such as social upheaval, the suffering of the people, and the aspiration of individuals, expressing their creative spirit and resolve to pursue a noble cause. Their works demonstrate strength, courage and determination to overcome great odds. With a melancholy and powerful style that was magnificent, unique, and distinctive of its age, Jian'an literature emerged as a unique genre and came to be viewed by later generations as an outstanding literary style, with Jian'an poetry particularly highly regarded.

引例 Citation：

◎暨建安之初，五言腾踊，文帝、陈思，纵辔以骋节；王、徐、应、刘，望路而争驱；并怜风月，狎池苑，述恩荣，叙酣宴，慷慨以任气，磊落以使才。（刘勰《文心雕龙·明诗》）

（到了建安初期，五言诗创作空前活跃，魏文帝曹丕和陈思王曹植驰骋文坛；王粲、徐干、应场、刘桢，随后奋力争先；他们都喜爱风月美景，游玩清池园囿，记述恩宠荣耀，叙写酣饮宴集，慷慨激昂地抒发豪气，洒脱直率地施展才情。）

In the early Jian'an era, the writing of poems in five-word lines gained unprecedented popularity, with Cao Pi (Emperor Wen of Wei) and Cao Zhi (Prince Si of Chen) dominating the literary scene. Other leading poets at the time include Wang Can, Xu Gan, Ying Yang, and Liu Zhen. They enjoyed beautiful scenery, particularly lakes and gardens as well as feasting and drinking; they reflected on the kindnesses they had received and past glories, and wrote about their sentiments and ambition in poems with passion and grace. (Liu Xie: *The Literary Mind and the Carving of Dragons*)

jiěbì 解蔽

Clear the Mind of Enigmas

解除认识上的蔽塞，以求获得对"道"的认识。"解蔽"一说出自《荀子》。荀子（前313？—前238）认为，人的良好的道德行为乃是基于人心对"道"的认识，但人心时常受到自身的好恶、欲求及各种外界因素的影响，从而形成片面的、狭隘的认识。要解除人心所受到的遮蔽，就需要锻炼心知

"道"的能力，使心处于"虚壹而静"的状态。

This term, from *Xunzi*, means to clear the mind of enigmas so that one may understand Dao. Xunzi (313?-238 BC) believes that man's moral integrity depends on his understanding of Dao. However, man's likes and dislikes, desires and external factors are likely to jaundice his understanding of Dao. To clear such enigmas, one needs to cultivate one's mind to keep it open, concentrated, and tranquil.

引例 Citation：

◎圣人知心术之患，见蔽塞之祸，故无欲无恶，无始无终，无近无远，无博无浅，无古无今。兼陈万物而中县（xuán）衡焉。是故众异不得相蔽以乱其伦也。(《荀子·解蔽》)

（圣人知晓心在认知上的弊病，看到心被蔽塞而带来的危害，因此不只注意欲求的一面，也不只注意厌恶的一面；不只注意起始，也不只注意终结；不只关注近处的事物，也不只关注遥远的事物；不只关注广博的方面，也不只关注浅显的方面；不只注意古代，也不只注意当下。把各种事物排列出来，在中间确定一个标准来加以判断。这样，事物间的众多差异就不会造成片面的认识而最终扰乱事物的秩序。）

Sages knew about the harm when one's mind is confused by enigmas. Attention should not be limited only to likes or dislikes, the beginnings or the ends of things, the things at hand or those far away, the extensive or the shallow aspects of things, the ancient or the present. Instead, all things need to be arrayed and then judged by a fixed standard. In this way, one can avoid one-sided knowledge of things and consequently misunderstanding of their order, due to the many differences between them. (*Xunzi*)

jīngqì 精气

Vital Energy

最精致细微的"气"。对"精气"较为详细的解释，最早见于《管子》。在《管子·内业》等篇的讨论中，"精气"指"气"中最精致细微的部分，是"道"的具体呈现。一切有形之物及人类都是由"精气"构成的。此外，人的生命、精神、智慧也被看作是"精气"作用的结果。

Vital energy refers to the finest and most subtle energy. The earliest detailed explanation of vital energy is found in *Guanzi*. According to the book, the finest and most subtle energy is a concrete manifestation of Dao. All things with shapes and all human beings are made up of vital energy; one's life, sense, and intelligence are also believed to derive from vital energy.

引例 Citations：

◎凡物之精，此则为生。下生五谷，上为列星。流于天地之间，谓之鬼神；藏于胸中，谓之圣人。(《管子·内业》)

（大凡事物所包含的"精气"，是事物得以生成的依据。在地生成五谷，在天生成众星。"精气"流转在天地之间，便称作鬼神；藏纳于胸中，便成为圣人的智慧。）

Everything is generated by its vital energy. Vital energy produces crops on the earth and forms stars in the sky. When vital energy comes between heaven and earth, it creates ghosts and spirits; when it goes into the heart of a human being, a sage is created. (*Guanzi*)

◎人之所以生者，精气也，死而精气灭。(王充《论衡·论死》)

（人之所以能够生存，依赖于精气，人死而精气消亡。）

People depend on vital energy for survival. When they die, their vital energy vanishes. (Wang Chong: *A Comparative Study of Different Schools of Learning*)

kèjǐ-fùlǐ 克己复礼

Restrain Yourself and Follow Social Norms

克制自己的言行以符合礼的要求。出自《论语》，是孔子（前551—前479）提出的实现仁德的基本方法。孔子认为，仁德的养成应以礼为标准。个人的言行应受到外在的礼的规范，但更重要的是通过约束自身的私欲，使自己的所见、所闻、言语、行为都符合礼的要求。能够做到"克己复礼"，就达成了仁德。

Restrain your words and deeds to comply with social norms. This term comes from *The Analects*. It is the fundamental method Confucius (551-479 BC) recommended for achieving benevolence. According to Confucius, social norms should be the standard for cultivating benevolence. Externally, your words and deeds should be subject to social norms, but more importantly, you should restrain your own selfish desires in order to see, listen, speak, and act within such norms. Once you can "restrain yourself and practice propriety," you will have achieved benevolence.

引例 Citation：

◎颜渊问仁。子曰："克己复礼为仁。一日克己复礼，天下归仁焉。为仁由己，而由人乎哉？"（《论语·颜渊》）

（颜渊请教何谓仁。孔子说："克制自己的言行以符合礼的要求就是仁。一旦能够克制自己的言行以符合礼的要求，天下都称许你的仁德。践行仁德依赖于自己，还要依赖别人吗？"）

Yan Yuan asked about benevolence. Confucius said, "To restrain yourself and practice propriety is benevolence. Once you can restrain yourself and practice propriety, everyone else will praise you for your benevolence. You must practice benevolence yourself; how can others practice it for you?" (*The Analects*)

kūdàn 枯淡

Dry Plainness

指诗文作品所呈现的质朴干枯、平和清淡的艺术风格。枯淡不是枯涩寡味、平庸浅薄，而是指外表看似干枯平淡、内里丰腴醇厚的一种表现手法，旨在用质朴平淡的语言和描写来表现丰富深刻的思想内容，创造出含蓄深邃、醇厚高远的意境。北宋初期，雕琢华艳的文风盛行，梅尧臣（1002—1060）、欧阳修（1007—1072）等人倡导诗文革新，标举平淡深邃的风格，认为诗歌的根本在于性情，无需刻意而为。苏轼（1037—1101）以陶渊明（365或372或376—427）、柳宗元（773—819）的诗歌为典范，进一步提出了"枯淡"的概念。"枯淡"与"平淡""淡泊""冲淡"等概念内涵接近，是道家冲和之美与儒家典雅之美的合流。

This refers to a literary style that appears plain and dry, mild and moderate. Here, dry and plain does not mean insipid, dull, common or shallow; rather, it suggests a means of expression that, while appearing prosaic, is rich in substance within. Its aim is to convey, in plain and simple language, a message that is not lacking in breadth or profundity and to create a deep and subtle, rich and far-reaching effect. In the early years of the Northern Song Dynasty, an ornate and sumptuous style prevailed in literature. Men of letters such as Mei Yaochen (1002-1060) and Ouyang Xiu (1007-1072) argued for literary renewal and endorsed a plain and penetrating style. They held that the essence of poetry lies in authenticity and true feeling and that there was no need to be too rhetorical. With the classical examples of Tao Yuanming's (365 or 372 or 376-427) and Liu Zongyuan's (773-819) poetry in mind, Su Shi (1037-1101) went on to put forth the notion of "dry plainness." It comes close in meaning to "calm," "unassuming," or "unpretentious" – a convergence of the peaceful and profound beauty of Daoism and the elegant beauty of Confucianism.

引例 Citations：

◎所贵乎枯淡者，谓其外枯而中膏，似淡而实美，渊明、子厚之流是也。若中边皆枯淡，亦何足道。（苏轼《评韩柳诗》）
（我之所以看重枯淡，是因为它形似干枯而内里丰腴，看似平淡而实际很美，像陶渊明、柳子厚等人的诗歌就是这样。如果中间、边侧都枯淡，那还有什么可称道的呢！）

I value the style of dry plainness because it looks withered and dry outside but is rich inside; it appears plain but is in fact beautiful. Poetry by such writers as Tao Yuanming and Liu Zongyuan is like this. If inner and outer were equally dry, why praise it? (Su Shi: A Critique of Poems by Han Yu and Liu Zongyuan)

◎故观之虽若天下之至质，而实天下之至华；虽若天下之至枯，而实天下之至腴。如彭泽一派，来自天稷者，尚庶几焉，而亦岂能全合哉！（包恢《答傅当可论诗》）
（所以，看起来虽像天下最质朴的，实际上却是天下最华美的；看起来虽像天下最枯槁的，实际上却是天下最丰腴的。像陶渊明等人的诗歌，自然天成，大致达到了这种境界，然而也不能完全符合啊！）

Therefore, what seems most plain in the world is in fact the most resplendent, and what seems most dry and withered is in fact the most fruitful. Poems by people like Tao Yuanming and his followers read naturally; they more or less achieved this artistic effect, though not completely! (Bao Hui: Reply to Fu Dangke's Discussion of Poetry)

kuángjuàn 狂狷

Proactive Versus Prudent

激昂进取与拘谨持守。孔子以"狂"和"狷"来指称两种为人处世的态度和作风。孔子（前551—前479）认为，理想的处事方式是不偏不倚，无过或不及。而"狂"和"狷"各有所偏："狂"则激昂进取，弘扬道义而不做任何妥协；"狷"则拘谨持守，谨慎退让但不失节操。二者虽有所偏颇，但都合乎道义，皆有可取之处。

Proactive and prudent were used by Confucius (551-479 BC) to refer to two opposing attitudes and styles of behavior. Proactive persons tend to be radical and won't make any compromise in upholding moral principles and justice. Prudent persons, on the other hand, tend to be cautious and ready to make compromise but without sacrificing moral integrity. Confucius believed that the ideal conduct in life is keeping to the mean, neither going too far nor falling short. While proactive and prudent may be extreme to some extent, both have their own advantages as both adhere to moral principles and justice.

引例 Citation：

◎子曰："不得中行而与之，必也狂狷乎？狂者进取，狷者有所不为也。"（《论语·子路》）

（孔子说："不能与遵循中道的人相交，也一定要结交狂者或狷者。狂者激昂进取，狷者不做有违道义的事。"）

Confucius said, "If one cannot make friends with those who adhere to the middle way, at least be close to aspiring or uninhibited minds. The former aims high whereas the latter never violates moral laws." (*The Analects*)

lǐqù 理趣

Philosophical Substance Through Artistic Appeal

指文学作品通过艺术形象而展示给人们的某种哲理和审美趣味，亦指读者通过对作品的阅读欣赏而领略到的其中所蕴含的哲理启示与审美趣味。魏晋南北朝出现的玄言诗崇尚玄理，宋人好以议论入诗，皆为后人诟病。因而有些诗歌评论家反对脱离艺术形象而单纯说"理"的创作理念，主张将"理"寄寓在艺术形象中，化为鲜活生动的审美趣味，所以称作理趣。这里的"理"是人生体悟，而非知识和学问，不能用逻辑概念去表达。这里的"趣"是一种审美情趣，是体悟人生哲理后的内心喜悦。"理趣说"将诗歌能否说理的争议转化为哲理与情趣相结合的理论主张，有助于辩证看待一切寄寓思考与体悟的文学作品。

This term refers to the philosophical substance of a work as well as its literary appeal conveyed to readers through its artistic image. In other words, it means the philosophical insights and aesthetic engagement that readers acquire through the process of appreciatively reading classic literary works. For example, poets of the Wei, Jin, or Southern and Northern dynasties were fond of entertaining abstruse schools of philosophy in their poems, while Song-dynasty poets often used poetry to comment on the society of their time. Both practices were treated as faults by some critics of later times. Some later critics even maintained that philosophical content should never figure into a poem apart from artistic images. Instead they insisted that the substantial content of the poem should be conveyed only by means of artistic images so that it could be grasped by readers through their appreciation of the work's artistic features, thus the term "substance through artistic appeal." *Li* (理) in this phrase refers to insights derived from the experience of life rather than bookish knowledge and learning. It is not something that can be acquired or expressed through logical argument. *Qu* (趣) refers to the aesthetic delight readers obtain when they acquire insight into life through reading classic literary works. This concept turns the dispute over whether poems could present logical arguments into a theory of the integration of reason and taste in poetic writing. It helps critics appreciate dialectically those literary works that contain both logic and insight.

引例 Citations：

◎ 盖古人于诗不苟作、不多作，而或一诗之出，必极天下之至精。状理则理趣浑然，状事则事情昭然，状物则物态宛然。（包恢《答曾子华论诗》）

（大约古人作诗，不轻易作，也不多作，只要创作一首诗，就一定追求天底下最好。说理则哲理与趣味浑然一体，叙事则事情的来龙去脉很明晰，写物则事物的形态让人感觉真切自然。）

Most likely, when writing poems, the classic poets neither wrote carelessly nor wrote many of them. Once they had decided to write a poem, they would strive to create the best work possible. As for philosophical substance, the argument and its aesthetic appeal should be well integrated; when it came to narration, the logic of the story was made perfectly clear, and descriptions were such that the thing described would appear natural and lifelike. (Bao Hui: *Letter to Zeng Zihua on Poetry*)

◎诗不能离理，然贵有理趣，不贵下理语。（沈德潜《清诗别裁集·凡例》）（写诗不能背离哲理，但贵在将哲理与审美趣味融为一体，不推崇直接写出哲理。）

A poem cannot avoid philosophical content, yet it is best to integrate the argument with aesthetic appeal. Direct argument is inappropriate for poetry. (Shen Deqian: *Collection of Poems in the Qing Dynasty*)

liǎngyí 两仪

Two Modes

事物生成与存在的两种仪则，是用以表现"八卦"生成过程的一个易学概念。《周易·系辞上》言:"《易》有太极，是生两仪，两仪生四象，四象生八卦。""太极"分化而形成相互匹配、对立的两面，即是"两仪"。就"两仪"的具体内容而言，古人有不同的理解：其一，从宇宙生成的角度来看，"两仪"或指天、地，或指阴、阳。其二，从占筮的角度来理解，"两仪"指由四十九根蓍草任意划分出的两组，或指画卦中分出的奇偶两画。

Things come into being and exist in two modes, which are used to describe how the eight trigrams are formed. As explained in *The Book of Changes*: "The

Book of Changes involve *taiji* (太极 the supreme ultimate), which produces two modes. The two modes generate the four images, and the four images give birth to the eight trigrams." *Taiji* divides itself into two mutually complementary but opposite parts, or modes. Ancient Chinese had different views as to what the modes represented. Some believed that from the point of view of the formation of the universe, the two modes could be understood as heaven and earth or as yin and yang. Others thought that as a term in divination, the two modes could refer to two groups formed by randomly dividing up 49 yarrow stalks used in divination, or the two lines, solid or broken, in the hexagrams of *The Book of Changes*.

引例 Citations：

◎混元既分，即有天地，故曰"太极生两仪"。(《周易·系辞上》孔颖达正义)

（混一的元气既已分化，即形成了天与地，所以《周易》称"太极生两仪"。）

Once the primordial chaos divided itself, there came into being heaven and earth. Therefore it is said in *The Book of Changes* that *taiji* (the supreme ultimate) gives birth to the two modes. (Kong Yingda: *Correct Meaning of The Book of Changes*)

◎分阴分阳，两仪立焉。(周敦颐《太极图说》)

（分化出了阴与阳，两仪就确立了。）

When yin and yang appeared, the two modes emerged. (Zhou Dunyi: The *Taiji Diagram Explained*)

lóng 龙

Chinese Dragon

传说中一种神异、祥瑞的动物，其形象综合了多种动物的特征：牛头、鹿角、虾眼、驴嘴、人须、蛇身、鹰爪等；能走、能飞、能游泳，能兴云布雨、善于变化，法力无边。它是中华民族最古老的图腾之一，秦汉以后成为帝王或皇室的象征，后又演化为汉民族及所有中国人共同的精神标记和文化符号。中国"龙"象征统合、强大、尊贵、威严、杰出、吉祥等，与西方神话传说中邪恶、贪婪的 dragon 有所区别。

The Chinese dragon is a mystique and auspicious animal in Chinese mythology, with its image having the features of a number of animals: bull's head, deer antlers, shrimp's eyes, donkey's mouth, human beard, snake's body, and eagle's claws. It can walk, fly, swim, and even raise clouds and make rain. It holds boundless supernatural powers and can transform itself into different creatures at will. As one of the oldest totems of the Chinese nation, the Chinese dragon became a symbol of the emperor or the imperial house after the Qin and Han dynasties. Later, it further evolved into a common spiritual and cultural symbol of the Han ethnic group and all Chinese people. In China, the dragon represents unity, power, reverence, dignity, excellence and good luck, which is quite opposite to the evil and greedy dragon in Western mythology and tradition.

引例 Citations：

◎龙，鳞虫之长。能幽能明，能细能巨，能短能长；春分而登天，秋分而潜渊。（许慎《说文解字·龙部》）

（龙，有鳞动物之首。能隐能显，能小能大，能短能长；春分时飞到天上去，秋分时潜隐在深水里。）

The most powerful among scaly animals, the Chinese dragon can hide itself or be visible, be small or huge, be short or long. At the Spring equinox it mounts into the sky, and at the Autumn equinox it hides deep in the water. (Xu Shen: *Explanation of Script and Elucidation of Characters*)

◎龙能大能小，能升能隐。大则兴云吐雾，小则隐介藏形；升则飞腾于宇宙之间，隐则潜伏于波涛之内。……龙之为物，可比世之英雄。（罗贯中《三国演义》第二十一回）

（龙能大能小，能飞能隐。若变大，就能兴起云雾；若变小，就能隐藏形体；若高飞，则能在宇宙间飞腾；若隐藏，则能在波涛内潜伏。……龙作为一种物，可以用来类比人世间的英雄。）

A Chinese dragon can be big or small, and it can soar or hide. When big, it raises clouds and spews mist. When small, it conceals its body and becomes invisible. When soaring, it flies up in space, and when hiding, it lies low in the waves… A true hero should act just like a Chinese dragon. (Luo Guanzhong: *Romance of the Three Kingdoms*)

luànshìzhīyīn 乱世之音

Music of an Age of Disorder

指动乱时代的音乐。儒家认为，音乐与社会政治相互联通，音乐能反映出一个国家的政治盛衰得失及社会风俗的变化。如果一个国家政治腐败、社会动荡，其音乐、诗歌等文艺作品一定充满了怨恨愤怒。统治者必须及时检讨并纠正政治弊端，以避免出现败亡的下场。

Confucian scholars believed that music interacts with both society and its political evolution; it also reflects the rise and decline of a state's political strength and changes of social customs. If a state suffers from political corruption and social turmoil, its music and poetry will be full of resentment and anger. Hearing such music and poetry, the ruler must promptly review his governance and correct abuse of power so as to avoid downfall.

引例 Citations：

◎是故治世之音安以乐，其政和；乱世之音怨以怒，其政乖；亡国之音哀以思，其民困。声音之道，与政通矣。(《礼记·乐记》)
（所以，太平时代的音乐祥和欢乐，这是因为政治宽和的缘故；动乱时代的音乐充满了怨恨与愤怒，这是因为政治混乱的缘故；国家将亡时的音乐充满了悲哀忧思，这是因为民众困苦不堪的缘故。音乐所反映出的道理，与一个国家的政治是相通的。）

Hence, the music in time of peace indicates serenity and happiness because of good governance. The music in time of disorder indicates dissatisfaction and anger because of political turmoil. The music of a state on the verge of collapse reveals sorrow and anxiety because its people are in distress. So there is a connection between the music of a state and its governance. (*The Book of Rites*)

◎郑卫之音，乱世之音也，比于慢矣。桑间濮上之音，亡国之音也。其政散，其民流，诬上行私而不可止也。(《礼记·乐记》)
（郑国和卫国的音乐，就是动乱时代的音乐，近乎轻慢无节制了。濮水岸边的桑间所流行的音乐，属于国家将亡时的音乐。它们反映出时政极端混乱，民众流离失所，臣下欺瞒君上、图谋私利而不可制止。）

The music of the states of Zheng and Wei was the music of an age of disorder, bordering on wantonness. The music of Sangjian on the Pushui River was typical of a failing state. The government was dysfunctional, the people were displaced, yet officials cheated on the ruler and pursued selfish gains with no one to stop them. (*The Book of Rites*)

mínxīn 民心

Will of the People

民众的共同心愿。指一个国家或地区的全体民众对触及他们共同利益、具有广泛社会性的问题、现象或事情所做出的一种评价性判断和看法。中国古人常以"天命"作为政权合法性及政策制定的依据和最高理念，但实际上则常以"民心"作为"天命"的主要来源、内容及表现形式，并将其视为治国理政的根本原则，认为民心的向背决定着国家、政权、政事的盛衰兴替。它是中华民本思想的核心。自古至今，凡开明有为的政治家，无不将"民心"视为最大的政治。

This term refers to the evaluative judgment or view of the people in a country or region, on an issue, phenomenon or incident which touches on their common interest and which has broad societal meaning. Ancient Chinese often took the "mandate of heaven" to be the basis and highest concept for the legitimacy of political authority and for policymaking, but in fact they often regarded the "will of the people" to be the principal source, content, and manifestation of the "mandate of heaven." They also considered it to be the fundamental principle of a country's governance, and thought that having or losing the will of the people determined the rise or fall of a country and political power as well as the development of state affairs. It is the core of the Chinese concept of the people as the foundation of the state. All enlightened Chinese statesmen past and present have regarded the "will of the people" to be the most important factor in governance.

引例 Citations：

◎民心惟本，厥作惟叶。(战国竹简（五）《厚父》)

（[国家好比一棵树。] 民众的意愿是树根，它决定着枝叶的生长与繁茂。）

(A country is like a tree.) Its root is the will of the people, which determines the growth and lushness of its leaves. (Houfu, from *Bamboo Slips of the Warring States Period*)

◎天矜于民。民之所欲，天必从之。(《尚书·泰誓上》)

（上天是爱惜民众的。民众的愿望，上天一定依从。）

Heaven loves the people and accedes to their wishes. (*The Book of History*)

◎政之所兴，在顺民心；政之所废，在逆民心。(《管子·牧民》)

（国家政权兴盛，是因为它顺应民心；国家政权废弛，是因为它违背民心。）

When the power of the state waxes, it is because it accords with the will of the people; when the power of the state wanes, it is because it goes against the will of the people. (*Guanzi*)

mínxīn-wéiběn 民心惟本

The People's Will Is the Foundation of the State.

民众的意愿、意志是政治的根本。出自战国竹简（五）《厚父》中所记载的商王（一说即太甲）与厚父（一说即伊尹）的一则对话，厚父对商王说："民心惟本，厥作惟叶。"字面意思是民心像树的根，而树根决定枝叶的生长与繁茂。其深层意思则是说民心是国家的根本，民心的向背最终决定国家或政权的盛衰兴替。古人认为，一个政权的合法性在于"顺天应人"，而"天意"以"民心"为基础或前提，只有顺应"民心"，国家才能长治久安。它与"民惟邦本"的思想是一致的。

The notion of the people's will being the foundation, or the "roots," of government comes from a dialogue between a king of the Shang Dynasty and Houfu (in a text found on bamboo slips of the Warring States Period). Houfu said to the king, "people's will is like the roots of a tree: they support the leaves." By that he meant that public support was the foundation of the state, and without it the state or political power would perish. The ancients believed that a government was legitimate so long as it "followed the mandate of heaven and complied with the wishes of the people." The people's wishes were a prerequisite of heaven's will, and only if the state complied with the people's wishes, would it enjoy lasting stability. This notion is identical to the concept that "people are the foundation of the state."

引例 Citations：

◎得天下有道，得其民，斯得天下矣。得其民有道，得其心，斯得民矣。得其

心有道，所欲与之聚之，所恶勿施尔也。(《孟子·离娄上》)

（得到天下有规律，得到百姓，就能得到天下。得到百姓有规律，得到民心，就能得到百姓。得到民心有规律，百姓想得到的，就替他们聚积起来；百姓所厌恶的，就不要施加于他们身上，如此罢了。）

There is a way to win all under heaven: if you win the people, you win all under heaven. There is a way to win the people: if you win their hearts, you win the people. There is a way to win their hearts: amass for them what they desire, do not impose on them what they detest, and it is as simple as that. (*Mencius*)

◎治国犹如栽树，本根不摇，则枝叶茂荣。(吴兢《贞观政要·政体》)

（治国就像栽树，树根坚实不动，枝叶自然生长繁茂。）

Governing a country is like planting a tree. If the roots are firm, the leaves and branches flourish. (Wu Jing: *Important Political Affairs of the Zhenguan Reign*)

◎民为邦本，未有本摇而枝叶不动者。(苏舜钦《诣匦（guǐ）疏》)

（民众是国家的根本，没听说根本摇动了而枝叶却不摇动的情况。）

The people are the foundation of the state. If the roots are not firm, the branches and leaves of the tree cannot but follow suit. (Su Shunqin: Memorial to the Emperor)

mín yǐ shí wéi tiān 民以食为天

Food Is of Primary Importance to the People.

民众将粮食看作天大的事情。"食"即粮食，泛指人类生存不可或缺的基本资源或物质条件；"天"比喻最重要的事物或主宰一切的根本因素。

古人认为，治国者不仅要知道百姓是君主的"天"、国家的"本"，而且要知道百姓的"天"是什么；粮食既是百姓糊口养家、安居乐业不可或缺的基本物质条件，当然也是任何领导集团招抚民众，保障民生不可或缺的基本资源。确保百姓能吃上饭、吃饱饭，确保基本生存资源的供应，是治国安民的一条底线。这是一个非常务实的政治理念。

The people consider food to be of the utmost importance. *Shi* (食 food) is a general term for the basic resources or material conditions essential to human life; *tian* (天 heaven) refers to the most important things or the basic elements which determine everything. Ancient Chinese believed that rulers not only had to understand that the ordinary people were the ruler's "heaven" and the "foundation" of the state, they also had to understand what the ordinary people's "heaven" was. Food is an indispensable basic material condition for the people to feed themselves, support their families, live peacefully, and fulfill stable jobs; of course it is also an indispensable basic material condition for a ruling group to mollify the people and ensure their livelihood. The bottom line for governing a country and helping its people is to guarantee the people food to eat and enough of it, and to guarantee the supply of basic resources needed for survival. This is an extremely pragmatic political concept.

引例 Citations：

◎［郦］食其（yìjī）因曰："臣闻之：'知天之天者，王事可成；不知天之天者，王事不可成。'王者以民为天，而民以食为天。"（《汉书·郦食其传》）

（郦食其于是说："我听说'知道什么是天的人可成就帝王之业，不知道什么是天的人不能成就帝王之业。'崇尚王道的帝王以百姓为天，而百姓以粮食为天。"）

Li Yiji then said, "I hear that those who understand the ways of heaven can accomplish the job of kings, while those who do not understand the ways of heaven cannot. Rulers who honor the kingly way regard the people as heaven, and the people regard food as heaven." (*The History of the Han Dynasty*)

◎国以民为本，民以食为天，衣其次也。(《三国志·吴书·陆凯传》)

(国家以百姓为根本，百姓以粮食为天，穿衣问题次之。)

The people are the foundation of a state, food is heaven to the people, and clothing is the next most important thing. (*The History of the Three Kingdoms*)

mínzhǔ 民主

Lord of the People / Democracy

本义为民之主（含为民做主之义），即君主或帝王；后也指官吏。古人认为，"民主"是"顺天应人"的产物；"民"与"主"是一个有机体，犹如人的身与心。近代以来，"民主"成为 democracy 的译词，主要指国家权力属于全体国民所有这一根本原则以及基于这一原则构成的政治制度和社会状态。民主的本质是人民当家做主，有管理国家与社会的权力，并在这一过程中能自由表达意见、维护自己的利益。民主以多数决定但同时尊重个人与少数人的权利为基本原则。其核心是公民的社会地位，是"人权"社会化的"实现方式"，也是构建美好社会的核心价值之一。

The term originally referred to the lord of the people, the one who ruled on their behalf, i.e., the monarch. Later on it also referred to government officials. The people of ancient times regarded the "lord of the people" as "following the mandate of heaven and complying with the wishes of the people." The people and their lord formed an organic whole like the human body and heart. In modern China, the term has become the Chinese equivalent of "democracy," mainly meaning the fundamental principle of state power belonging to all of the people and also the political system and social conditions based on that principle. In essence democracy is government by the people who are able to exercise the right of managing state and society, and who, in this process, can freely express their opinions and safeguard their interests. Democracy is based on the principle of decision by the majority with due respect for the rights of individuals and the minority. Democracy is designed to safeguard the social status of citizens. It is a socialized form of human rights, and one of the core values conducive to a good society.

引例 Citations：

◎自古已来，能除民害为百姓所归者，即民主也。(《三国志·魏书·武帝纪》裴松之注引《魏氏春秋》)

(自古以来，能够铲除为害百姓的祸端而使天下百姓归顺的人，就是百姓的君王。)

Since ancient times, one who could save the people from harm and enjoy their allegiance was the lord of the people. (Pei Songzhi: *Annotations on The History of the Three Kingdoms*)

◎民以君为心，君以民为体。……心以体全，亦以体伤。君以民存，亦以民亡。(《礼记·缁衣》)

(百姓将国君看作人的心，国君将百姓看作人的身体。……心因为有身体而得以保全，也因为身体受损而损伤。国君因为有百姓而得以存在，也因为百姓反对而灭亡。)

To the people the sovereign ruler is as their heart; to the ruler the people are as his body… The heart is safe because of the body, while it suffers when the body is wounded. So the ruler is preserved by the people and perishes when the people turn against him. (*The Book of Rites*)

qīngcí-lìjù 清词丽句

Refreshing Words and Exquisite Expressions

指立意新颖、情感真挚、物象鲜明而语言清新美妙的诗句。"清"主要针对堆砌辞藻和典故而言,不仅指词句清新自然,还指格调高雅而意境淡远;"丽"指的也不是词语本身的华丽,而是指尽脱俗气,物象鲜明而有真情。作为一个诗学术语,它实际是指包括语言风格在内的诗歌整体风格。

This term refers to verses original in theme, sincere in feeling, distinctive in image, and refreshing in diction. "Refreshing" stands opposed to ornate phrases and excessive literary quotations, and indicates both fresh and natural expressions as well as elegant style and subtle aesthetic conception. What "exquisite" indicates is not that the wording itself is resplendent, but that there is complete freedom from vulgarity, and that the imagery is sharp with real sentiments. As a poetic term, it refers to the general feature of a poem, including its linguistic style.

引例 Citation:

◎不薄今人爱古人,清词丽句必为邻。(杜甫《戏为六绝句》其五)
(学诗既要效法古代名家,也不能轻视当世才俊;一切清新自然、鲜明动人的作品，定要加以亲近揣摩。）

In writing poems, one should emulate past eminent poets. At the same time, he should not ignore contemporary talents either. Every refreshing, natural, distinct, and impressive work should be studied closely. (Du Fu: Six Playful Quatrains)

rénmín-àiwù 仁民爱物

Have Love for the People, and Cherish All Things

仁爱百姓，爱惜万物。这里的"物"泛指一切禽兽草木，而"爱"意思是取之有时、用之有节。它是孟子（前372？—前289）提出的一种思想。孟子认为，人类对待自己亲人的态度是亲爱，对待百姓的态度是仁爱，对待动植物的态度是爱惜，这是自然形成的情感差异。爱虽然有亲疏差等，但君子能以"亲亲"为原点，推己及人，广被万物，即由爱亲人进而仁爱百姓，进而爱惜万物。它是一种源于家族本位而又超越家族本位，甚至超越人类本位、遍及万事万物的博大的爱，是达成人自身、人与人、人与自然关系和谐完满的基本原理。张载（1020—1077）的"民胞物与"思想与此不无渊源。

The term means to have love for the people, and cherish all things in the world. Here *wu* (物) includes plants and animals, while *ai* (爱) implies using them in a measured and appropriate way. This was first proposed by Mencius (372?-289 BC) who differentiated natural emotions as: a love for close family, a broad compassion for other people, and a sense of cherishing for plants and animals. The love could be close or distant, but a person of virtue always begins with love of close relatives, which then extends to other people and eventually to all things in the world. Though this feeling starts within the family, it should extend beyond it, even beyond the human race to include plants and animals, to become a broad love. The goal is to achieve harmony within oneself, with others and with nature. Zhang Zai's (1020-1077) concept that "all people are my brothers and sisters, and all things are my companions" is very similar.

引例 Citations：

◎孟子曰："君子之于物也，爱之而弗仁；于民也，仁之而弗亲。亲亲而仁民，仁民而爱物。"（《孟子·尽心上》）

（孟子说："君子对于万物，爱惜却说不上仁爱；对于百姓，仁爱却说不上亲爱。君子亲爱亲人，因而仁爱百姓；仁爱百姓，因而爱惜万物。"）

Mencius said, "Men of virtue cherish all things but this is not benevolent love, have compassion for others but this is not love of family. Men of virtue love and care for their loved ones, they are therefore kind to other people. When they are kind to people, they treasure everything on earth." (*Mencius*)

◎凡人之生，皆得天地之理以成性，得天地之气以成形，我与民物，其大本乃同出一源。若但知私己而不知仁民爱物，是于大本一源之道已悖而失之矣。（曾国藩《日课四条·同治十年金陵节署中日记》）

（大凡人出生时，都禀受了天地的"理"而成就本性，都得到了天地的"气"而成就形象。我与万民、万物在根本上是同出一源的。假如我只知自私自利而不知仁民爱物，那么就和我与万民万物同根同源这个道理相背离而失去自我了。）

At birth, all humans in accordance with nature's laws are bestowed with natural tendencies, and derive their forms from vital force *qi*. I come from the same origins as all people and the myriad things on earth. If I care only about my selfish interests and ignore love for all people and things, then I turn my back on our common origins, and lose my sense of self. (Zeng Guofan: On the Four Aspects of Daily Self-improvement, Diary Written at the Residence of Jinling)

sānbùxiǔ 三不朽

Set Moral Examples, Perform Great Deeds, and Spread Noble Ideas

世间三种永不磨灭或永远受人怀念、称颂的业绩,即"立德""立功""立言",也称"三立"。最高的是"立德",确立典范的道德,垂范后世;其次是"立功",建立伟大的功业,为国家百姓兴利除害;最后是"立言",提出包含真知灼见的言论,以启迪后人,或撰文著述,成一家之言。据《左传》记载,"三不朽"由春秋时期鲁国叔孙豹提出。在叔孙豹看来,个人或家族的私利,无论是财富还是官爵、地位,总会随时间的推移而逐渐消失。只有真正利于国家百姓的"德""功""言",才能长期流传而不朽。"三不朽"后来成为古代士人及每一位有抱负的人的毕生追求。

This term refers to three great accomplishments that are forever remembered and eulogized by the people. The first and foremost is to set a high moral standard for people of later generations to follow. The second is to perform meritorious deeds, bringing good to the country and the people and rooting out evils. The third is to put forth noble ideas or establish them as a way of thinking through writing them down. According to *Zuo's Commentary on The Spring and Autumn Annals*, these great accomplishments were proposed by Shusun Bao from the State of Lu in the Spring and Autumn Period. In Shusun's opinion, private benefits that individuals or families have, such as wealth, official ranking, and social status, will disappear with the passage of time. Only the great accomplishments that benefit the country and the people, including setting out high moral standards, performing great deeds, and inseminating noble ideas, can be passed on for eternity. These three great accomplishments have been the lifelong pursuit of ancient Chinese literati and people of noble aspirations.

引例 Citation：

◎豹闻之，大上有立德，其次有立功，其次有立言。虽久不废，此之谓不朽。(《左传·襄公二十四年》)

(我听说，最高的境界是确立典范的道德，其次是建立伟大的功业，再次是倡立正确的言论。三者即使经过漫长的岁月也不会废弃，这就是所谓的"不朽"。)

I hear that the noblest pursuit is to set a moral example; the second is to perform great deeds; and the third is to advocate noble ideas. These great accomplishments will last and never be abandoned by people despite the passage of time. (*Zuo's Commentary on The Spring and Autumn Annals*)

shānshuǐshī 山水诗

Landscape Poetry

一种以描写山水名胜为主要题材的诗歌流派。主要摹写自然山川的秀美壮丽并借以抒发闲情逸致，特点是写景状物逼真细致，语言表达富丽清新。东晋时期，南渡的士大夫在自然山水中寻求精神抚慰和解脱，激发了山水诗创作的灵感。其开创者是晋末宋初的大诗人谢灵运（385—433），他把自然美景引入诗歌创作,将诗歌从枯燥乏味的玄理中解放出来,后经谢朓(tiǎo,464—499)、何逊(?—518?)、阴铿等人的创作实践而逐步成为诗歌史上的一个重要诗派。到唐代特别是盛唐时期,山水诗的创作更是蔚为大观,涌现出王维(701?—761)、孟浩然(689—740)等著名山水诗人,中唐时期的刘长卿(?—789?)、韦应物(737?—791)、柳宗元(773—819)等人的创作也有特色。山水诗开启了新的诗歌风貌,标志着一种新的审美观念的产生。

Landscape poetry, as the name suggests, describes the beauty and charm of natural scenery, and landscape poets express their emotions through extolling the enchanting scenery. Landscape poetry is characterized by vivid description of sights with rich and refreshing language. During the Eastern Jin Dynasty, scholars who had fled war-torn homes in the north sought solace and escape in nature in the south, and this found expression in poetic description of mountain and river scenes. Xie Lingyun (385-433), a great poet of the late Eastern Jin and early Song Dynasty of the Southern Dynasties, created this poetic style. He introduced the depiction of natural beauty into poetry writing, freeing poetry from bland and insipid moral preaching. Further developed by Xie Tiao (464-499), He Xun (?-518?), Yin Keng, and others, landscape poetry became an important literary school. It gained prominence in the Tang Dynasty, especially in the prime of Tang, during which such landscape poets like Wang Wei (701?-761) and Meng Haoran (689-740) distinguished themselves. Mid-Tang poets including Liu Changqing (?-789?), Wei Yingwu (737?-791), and Liu Zongyuan (773-819) also became famous for writing landscape poems. This gave rise to a new form of expression in poetry and a new trend of aesthetic appreciation.

引例 Citation：

◎宋初文咏，体有因革。庄老告退，而山水方滋；俪采百字之偶，争价一句之奇，情必极貌以写物，辞必穷力而追新，此近世之所竞也。（刘勰《文心雕龙·明诗》）

（[南朝]宋初期的诗文，风格上有继承有变革，表现老庄思想的玄言诗退出诗坛，而山水诗正在崛起；文人用数百字的骈偶堆砌辞藻，为了某一句的新奇而攀比争胜，描绘外物务求穷形极胜，遣词造句必定竭力追求新异，这就是近代人们所竞相追逐的目标。）

The literature and poetry of the early Song Dynasty of the Southern Dynasties saw some changing trend: metaphysical poetry implicating Laozi and Zhuangzi's thoughts declined and landscape poetry gained in popularity. Poets sometimes used a few hundred words of parallel prose just to describe a scene, or competed with each other in writing an unusual line. In describing scenes, they tried to depict every detail; in composing a literary work, they racked their brains to achieve what is unusual. This has become the current trend in literary writing. (Liu Xie: *The Literary Mind and the Carving of Dragons*)

shàngtóng 尚同

Conform Upwardly

指是非标准同一于上级统治者。"尚同"是墨家的基本主张之一。墨子（前468？—前376）认为，在没有国家、政治之时，人们会因为是非标准的混乱而导致相互非议、争斗，造成彼此之间的伤害。因此主张立贤能之人为天子及各级官吏，所有人的言行是非标准皆服从于上级，并最终同一于天子；天子则服从于上天的要求。墨家认为"尚同"是实现天下大治的重要手段。

This term means conforming to the superior in applying standards for right and wrong. It is one of the basic positions of the Mohist school. Mozi (468?-376 BC) believed that in the absence of a state and political power, confusion over right and wrong would give rise to conflict and fighting, causing harm to the antagonists. Therefore, he held that worthy and talented men should be the Son of Heaven and his officials at various levels. Everyone should adopt their superior's standards for judging right and wrong in words and deeds, and ultimately follow the ruler's standards. The sovereign ruler himself should submit to Heaven's will. The Mohists believed that conforming upwardly was an important means to ensure great order under heaven.

引例 Citation：

◎ 上之所是，必亦是之。上之所非，必亦非之。己有善，傍荐之。上有过，规谏之。尚同乎其上，而毋有下比之心。(《墨子·尚同中》)

(上位者所肯定的，必须也加以肯定。上位者所否定的，必须也加以否定。自己有好的主张，就想法进谏给上位者。上位者有过错，就规劝他。是非标准都同一于上位者，而不要有与下位者比附的想法。)

What your superior affirms, you must also affirm. What your superior rejects, you must also reject. If you have a good idea, manage to go to your superior and recommend it. If your superior commits an error, admonish him and remonstrate. Upwardly you should conform to your superior, not to your subordinates. (*Mozi*)

shàngxián 尚贤

Exalt the Worthy

崇尚贤才。中国古代很多学派都提出过"尚贤"或类似的主张。"尚贤"要求执政者崇尚贤能之士，并依据其德行、才能赋予相应的职权，使其在国家治理中充分发挥其作用。良好的德才应成为选任官吏的优先原则。对儒家而言，"尚贤"是对"亲亲"原则的有益补充。墨家则将其作为实现"尚同"之治的重要条件。

In ancient China, many schools of thought advocated "exalting the worthy" or similar ideas. They asked those in power to employ worthy and able men and make effective use of them in governance by assigning them positions and responsibilities corresponding to their virtues. Virtue and talent were to be the first and foremost criterion in selecting officials. To the Confucians, empowering the virtuous and able was a useful complement to loving and caring for kinsmen. To the Mohists, empowering the virtuous and able was an important prerequisite for governance that "conforms upwardly."

引例 Citations：

◎故尚贤使能，等贵贱，分亲疏，序长幼，此先王之道也。(《荀子·君子》)
（因此崇尚贤才任用能人，使尊贵与卑贱有差等，使亲近与疏远有区分，使年长与年幼有次序，这就是先王遵行的原则。）

Thus, exalting the worthy and employing the capable, ranking the noble and the lowly, differentiating those close and distant, assigning precedence to old and young: this is the principle followed by former kings. (*Xunzi*)

◎故古者圣王甚尊尚贤，而任使能，不党父兄，不偏贵富，不嬖（bì）颜色。（《墨子·尚贤中》）

（因此古代的圣王十分推崇尚贤的原则，而任使贤能之人，不结党于父亲兄弟，不偏私于尊贵富有之人，不宠爱容貌姣好之人。）

Therefore, in antiquity the sage kings greatly honored the principle of exalting the worthy. They employed the virtuous and capable, forming no cliques with their fathers and brothers, showing no partiality to the rich and noble, nor favoring those with handsome features. (*Mozi*)

shēngshēng 生生

Perpetual Growth and Change

生生不息的变化。出自《周易·系辞上》。《周易》所言"生生"包含两层含义：其一，就万物的存在而言，"生生"指天地万物处于永恒的生成、变化之中，阴阳的交互作用构成了"生生"的内在动力。"生生"是天地万物的根本属性，也是道德之善行的来源。其二，就占筮而言，"生生"指奇画与偶画相交错，卦爻之象处于不断变化之中。

The term stands for perpetual change. According to *The Book of Changes*, *shengsheng* (生生) can be understood at two levels. First, in regard to the existence of all things, it is the interaction of yin and yang that drives the process of the endless cycle of birth, rebirth, and change of heaven, earth, and all things. This process is a fundamental attribute of the universe, and the source of ethical behavior. Second, as a term in divination, it refers to the alternation of yin and yang lines and the fact that all elements in the symbol system of *The*

Book of Changes are in a perpetual state of change.

引例 Citations：

◎生生之谓易。(《周易·系辞上》)
(生生不息，称之为"易"。)

One generation gives life to another generation in perpetual change. (*The Book of Changes*)

◎生生之谓易，是天之所以为道也。天只是以生为道，继此生理者，即是善也。(《二程遗书》卷二上)
(生生不息的变化，就是天道的内容。天只是以生生不息为原则，秉承此生生不息之理的，就是善。)

Continued growth and perpetual change is essence of the way of heaven. Heaven follows this principle, and kindness is guided by this principle. (*Writings of the Cheng Brothers*)

shèngtángzhīyīn 盛唐之音

Poetry of the Prime Tang Dynasty

指唐玄宗开元（713—741）、天宝（742—756）年间的诗歌创作与艺术成就。与初唐、中唐、晚唐时期的诗歌相对应。这一时期是"安史之乱"前唐帝国的黄金时代，当时，社会稳定、政治清明、经济繁荣，南北文化融合，中外交通发达，这一切为"盛唐之音"营造了很好的社会氛围和文化基础。在唐诗初、盛、中、晚四个阶段中，盛唐最短，但艺术成就最为辉煌，被后人誉为"盛唐气象"。这一时期，不但出现了诗仙李白（701—762）、诗圣杜甫

（712—770），而且还出现了张说（yuè，667—731）、张若虚、张九龄（673或678—740）、孟浩然（689—740）、王维（701？—761）、高适（700？—765）、岑参（shēn，715—770）、王昌龄（？—756？）、王之涣（688—742）、崔颢（？—754）、李颀（？—753？）、王翰等一大批卓有成就的诗人。他们赞美山川，向往功业，抒发个人情志，记述社会现实，诗风豪迈浑厚，意境宏阔高远，语言清新天然，富有生命活力与进取精神，创造了中国古典诗歌的最高成就。就诗派而论，这一时期则有山水田园诗派、边塞诗派等。

This term refers to the poetic creation and achievements during the Kaiyuan (713–742) and Tianbao (742–756) reign periods of Emperor Xuanzong of the Tang Dynasty, as compared with poetic writing in the early Tang, mid-Tang, and late Tang periods. This period, marked by good governance, prosperity, and stability, was a golden era for the great Tang empire before it was disrupted by the An Lushan and Shi Siming Rebellion. There was cultural infusion between the north and south, and travels to and from the outside world were frequent. All this made it possible for artistic creation to blossom. Of all the four periods of poetic creation, i.e., the early Tang, the prime Tang, the mid-Tang, and the late Tang, the prime Tang was the shortest, but its artistic attainment was most remarkable. This period produced legendary poet Li Bai (701-762) and poetic genius Du Fu (712-770) as well as a galaxy of outstanding poets such as Zhang Yue (667-731), Zhang Ruoxu, Zhang Jiuling (673 or 678-740), Meng Haoran (689-740), Wang Wei (701?-761), Gao Shi (700?-765), Cen Shen (715-770), Wang Changling (?-756?), Wang Zhihuan (688-742), Cui Hao (?-754), Li Qi (?-753?), and Wang Han. These poets extolled natural scenery, expressed noble aspirations, and depicted real life. Their writing style was both vigorous and unrestrained. They were broad in vision and were adept at using fresh, natural language, and their poems were full of power, vigor and an enterprising spirit. Their poems represented the highest attainment in classical Chinese poetry. This period also saw the thriving of the natural landscape school and the frontier school in poetry writing.

引例 Citations：

◎盛唐诸公之诗，如颜鲁公书，既笔力雄壮，又气象浑厚。(严羽《答出继叔临安吴景仙书》)

(盛唐诸多诗人的诗作，好比颜真卿的书法作品一样，笔力既雄壮感人，气象又质朴厚重。)

Works of many poets during the prime of the Tang Dynasty struck readers with their touching, powerful expression and simple yet dignified style, just like the calligraphy of Yan Zhenqing. (Yan Yu: Letter in Reply to Uncle Wu Jingxian in Lin'an)

◎盛唐气象浑成，神韵轩举。(胡应麟《诗薮·内编五》)

(盛唐时期的诗歌气象浑然一体、天然生成，其精神气韵也就自然昂扬飞举。)

Poetry in the prime of the Tang Dynasty is noted for being expressive, smooth and natural, creating a soaring and uplifting spirit. (Hu Yinglin: *An In-depth Exploration of Poetry*)

shìdézhěchāng, shìlìzhěwáng 恃德者昌，恃力者亡

Those Who Rely on Virtue Will Thrive; Those Who Rely on Force Will Perish.

依靠道义的就会兴旺，依靠暴力的就会消亡。见于《史记·商君列传》引《尚书》。"德"即道义、恩德、德行，"力"即强力、暴力、武力。受儒家政治伦理思想影响，中国人自古提倡"王道"（以德服人），反对"霸道"（以力压人）。认为以德服人才能使人心悦诚服，从而形成合力，使事业兴旺发达；而以力压人只能使人被迫屈从，不能达成真实持久的和谐与团结。管理一单位如此，治理一国家如此，处理国与国之间的关系亦如此。作为处理国与国之间关系的原则，其含义可以诠释为：穷兵黩武、弱肉强食有违文明发展，只有坚守道义、互信互谅才能造就世界的持久和平与安全。

Relying on moral strength will bring prosperity, whereas relying on violence will bring doom. The saying is described in *The Book of History* (as cited in *Records of the Historian*). *De* (德) refers to morals, grace, and integrity. *Li* (力) refers to coercion, violence, and military power. Under the influence of the political and ethical principles of the Confucian school, since ancient times the Chinese people have been advocating benevolent governance virtue (winning over people with benevolence) as opposed to rule by force (wielding power over people), believing that only by relying on benevolence can the ruler hope to win people's hearts and minds, resulting therefore in a positive synergy that brings about prosperity. Rule by force, on the other hand, can merely coerce people into submission, but cannot achieve genuine and lasting harmony and unity. This is true not only in managing an entity or governing a country, but also in handling relationships among countries. As a principle for managing international relations, the term suggests that wanton engagement in military action or attempting to completely dominate others are incompatible with the development of civilization. Only by observing moral principles and trusting one another can sustainable peace and security be achieved in the world.

引例 Citations：

◎德，国家之基也，有基无坏。(《左传·襄公二十四年》)
（德行，是国和家存在的根基，根基有了，国和家才不会被毁坏。）

Virtue is the foundation that supports a state and a family. Only upon this foundation can a state and a family stay invincible. (*Zuo's Commentary on The Spring and Autumn Annals*)

◎孟子曰："以力假仁者霸，霸必有大国；以德行仁者王，王不待大……以力服人者，非心服也，力不赡也；以德服人者，中心悦而诚服也。"(《孟子·公孙丑上》)

（孟子说："凭借强力而假托仁义的人可以称霸，称霸一定以大国作基础；依靠德行施行仁义的人可以称王，称王却不一定非大国不可……依靠强力使他人服从，他们并不是真心服从，而是力量不足以抗拒；通过德行而令人服从，他们是内心喜悦而诚心服从。"）

Mencius said, "One who seizes throne by force in the name of benevolence and justice needs a big state as his power base. One who ascends the throne by upholding morality and benevolence may not necessarily have a big state as his base… Coercion can bring people in line not because they are willing, but because they do not have the strength to resist; it is virtue that will persuade others to gladly and willingly follow." (*Mencius*)

◎ 为天下及国，莫如以德，莫如行义。以德以义，不赏而民劝，不罚而邪止。(《吕氏春秋·上德》)

(治理天下和国家，没有什么比得上德政，也没有什么比得上道义。采用德政和道义，不需赏赐民众就得到劝勉，不需惩罚邪恶就得到制止。)

Nothing is more important than benevolence and moral integrity in ruling a country and its people. When benevolence and morality are practiced, people will behave without any need for financial or material incentives. Evils will be inhibited without any need for punishment. (*Master Lü's Spring and Autumn Annals*)

sìxiàng 四象

Four Images

"八卦"生成过程中由"两仪"分化出的四种物象或特性。《周易·系辞上》言："《易》有太极，是生两仪，两仪生四象，四象生八卦。""两仪"继续分化形成相互区别而又相互关联的四种物象或特性，就是"四象"。对于"四象"的具体内容，古人有着不同的理解：其一，从万物生成的角度来看，"四象"或指春、夏、秋、冬四时，或指金、木、水、火四种基本元素。其二，从占筮的角度来理解，"四象"或指揲（shé）分蓍草时每组被分出的四根蓍草，或指画卦时所确定的太阴、太阳、少阴、少阳等四种爻象。

This term means the four images, or features of the four images, which are engendered through the division of the two modes in the process of the formation of the eight trigrams. As explained in *The Book of Changes*, "Changes involve *taiji* (太极 the supreme ultimate), which produces two modes. The two modes generate the four images, and the four images generate the eight trigrams." The four images are distinct from one another while also mutually related. There was no agreement among ancient scholars with regard to what the four images represent. From the point of view of the coming into being of all things, the four images might stand for the four seasons: spring, summer, autumn, and winter; or four basic elements: metal, wood, water, and fire. Alternatively, as a term in divination, the four images could refer to the four stalks in each group when the divination stalks are divided in a fortune-telling exercise, or to four line images for divination: greater yin, greater yang, lesser yin, and lesser yang.

引例 Citations：

◎大衍之数五十，其用四十有九。分而为二以象两，挂一以象三，揲之以四以象四时。(《周易·系辞上》)

(用来广泛推演变化的数是五十，使用的有四十九根蓍草。将这些蓍草分为两份，以象征"两仪"。从其中一份抽出一根蓍草，以象征天、地、人"三才"。其余蓍草则每四根为一组进行划分，以象征"四时"。)

The total number of divination stalks is fifty; those that are used are forty-nine. These are divided into two groups representing the pair of modes. One stalk is taken from one group to represent the three elements of heaven, earth, and man, and the rest are counted out in fours to represent the four seasons. (*The Book of Changes*)

◎"两仪生四象"者，谓金木水火，禀天地而有，故云"两仪生四象"。(《周易·系辞上》孔颖达正义)

(所谓"两仪生四象"，是指金木水火四种基本元素，禀受于天地而存有，所以说"两仪生四象"。)

The four images generated by the two modes refer to metal, wood, water, and fire. They come into existence thanks to heaven and earth, and therefore it is said that the two modes generate the four images. (Kong Yingda: *Correct Meaning of The Book of Changes*)

Tàikāng tǐ 太康体

The Taikang Literary Style

西晋初年和中期大约三十多年时间里的诗歌风格，指晋武帝（236-290）太康（280—289）年间以左思（250？—305？）、潘岳（247—300）、陆机（261—303）等人为代表的诗体。与建安（196—220）时代积极进取、昂扬向上的诗风不同，太康诗人讲究辞藻华丽和对偶工整，诗歌技巧更臻精美。其中，左思的作品语言质朴，但内容充实，气势雄浑，在太康诗风中独树一帜。

This term refers to a poetic style popular for about 30 years from the early to mid-Western Jin Dynasty, particularly in the Taikang era (280–289) during the reign of Emperor Wu (236-290). Among the poets of this tradition were Zuo Si (250?-305?), Pan Yue (247-300), and Lu Ji (261-303). Taikang poets focused excessively on the use of rhetorical description, verbal parallelism, and refined poetic techniques, representing an abrupt departure from the Jian'an (196-220) poetry with its passion, boldness, and vitality. Standing out among the Taikang poets was Zuo Si, who used plain language, but whose works had substance and were imbued with passion and strength.

引例 Citation：

◎太康中，三张、二陆、两潘、一左，勃尔复兴，踵武前王，风流未沫，亦文章之中兴也。（钟嵘《诗品》卷上）
（西晋太康时期，张载、张协、张亢、陆机、陆云、潘岳、潘尼和左思，突然复兴建安时期的兴盛局面，追寻前代杰出者的足迹，这是建安文学的风流未尽，也是诗文的中兴啊！）

In the Taikang era of the Western Jin Dynasty, scholars including Zhang Zai, Zhang Xie, Zhang Kang, Lu Ji, Lu Yun, Pan Yue, Pan Ni, and Zuo Si revived the literary legacy of the Jian'an period by following the footsteps of the masters of that period. It signalled the continuation and beauty of the Jian'an style and a resurgence of poetry writing. (Zhong Rong: *The Critique of Poetry*)

tì 悌

Fraternal Duty

弟弟对兄长的顺从与敬爱，也作"弟"。在言行上，"悌"要求为人弟者顺从、遵循兄长的教导与命令。"悌"应植根于弟弟内心对兄长的亲爱与敬重。儒家常将"悌"与"孝"并称，认为"孝悌"是个人德行养成的基础，并将其作为维系与强化家庭伦理乃至政治秩序的根本。

Fraternal duty is obedience to, and love and respect for one's elder brother. To observe this, the younger brother must follow an elder brother's guidance and orders. Fraternal duty should be rooted in the heartfelt love and respect for an elder brother. Confucians often speak of "fraternal duty" and "filial piety" together, believing that together they are the foundation for cultivating personal moral integrity, and are the basis for maintaining and strengthening family ethics, extending even to the political order.

引例 Citations:

◎ 有子曰:"其为人也孝弟(tì),而好犯上者,鲜(xiǎn)矣;不好犯上,而好作乱者,未之有也。君子务本,本立而道生。孝弟也者,其为仁之本与!"(《论语·学而》)

(有子说:"一个人为人处世孝敬父母、敬爱兄长,却喜欢触犯上级,这是很少见的;不喜欢触犯上级,而喜欢作乱的,这是从来没有的。君子致力于为人处世的根本,根本确立了,符合道义的言行即可产生。孝悌,就是仁德的根本。")

Youzi said, "Of those who practice filial piety and fraternal duty, few are likely to offend their superiors. Of those who are unlikely to offend their superiors, none have been fond of stirring up trouble. A man of virtue is devoted to the fundamentals of good behavior. That being established, words and deeds are produced in accordance with moral principles. Filial piety and fraternal duty are the basis of benevolence." (*The Analects*)

◎ 孝者,所以事君也;弟者,所以事长也;慈者,所以使众也。(《礼记·大学》)

(孝,可以用来事奉君主;悌,可以用来事奉长者;慈,可以用来任使民众。)

Filial piety is practiced in service of the sovereign. Fraternal duty is practiced in service of elders and senior officials. Kindness is practiced in directing the populace. (*The Book of Rites*)

tiānjīng-dìyì 天经地义

Natural Rules and Orderliness

天地的规则与秩序。据《左传》的记载，郑国子产（？—前522）提出了"天经地义"之说，以解释礼的本质及依据。在子产看来，天地的运行遵循着恒常的规则，并呈现出稳定的秩序，具有最高的合理性。人应效法于天地，符合"天经地义"的言行与秩序即是合理的、正当的。礼对人的言行及人伦秩序的规定，正是"天经地义"的体现。"天经地义"一词后来被广泛地用以描述各种事物的正当性及不容置疑的道理。

Literally, this term means the rules and orderliness of heaven and earth. According to *Zuo's Commentary on The Spring and Autumn Annals*, Zichan (?-522 BC) of the State of Zheng proposed the concept to explain the essence and justification of rites. Zichan believed that the movements of heaven and earth followed eternal rules that created a consistent and rational order. Man too should imitate this in word and deed in an orderly, rational, and proper way. The constraints that rites place on human behavior, and the resulting social ethics and harmony are all manifestations of these laws of nature. The expression later came to mean anything that is proper, or any reasoning that is justified.

引例 Citation：

◎夫礼，天之经也，地之义也，民之行也。(《左传·昭公二十五年》)
（礼是天地运行的法则，民众行为的规范。）

Rites represent the rules governing the movement of heaven and earth as well as the code of conduct for the people. (*Zuo's Commentary on The Spring and Autumn Annals*)

tiānshí dìlì rénhé 天时地利人和

Opportune Time, Geographic Advantage, and Unity of the People

"天时"本指作战时的有利气候，泛指时间上的各种有利条件，包括天气、时机、机遇等；"地利"本指作战时的有利地形，泛指空间上的各种有利条件，包括地形、地势、区位等；"人和"本指得到人们拥护，上下同心，团结一致，泛指人的优势。古人认为，它们是事关成败的三种最重要的因素；而且"天时不如地利，地利不如人和"，其中起决定作用的是"人和"。它反映了中国人考虑问题的三个基本向度——时间（时机）、空间（环境）和人，体现"以人为本"的基本理念。

"Opportune time," which originally referred to the favorable weather at the time of war, now generally refers to various temporal advantages, including weather, timing, opportunity, and so on. "Geographic advantage," which originally referred to advantageous positions in battle, now refers to generally various favorable spacial conditions, including terrain, position, location, and such. "Unity of the people," which originally referred to popular support, unity of all ranks, and societal solidarity, now refers in general to advantages in personnel. Ancient Chinese believed that these three were the most important factors for success. Among them, "unity of the people" is decisive because "opportune time is not as valuable as geographic advantage, and geographic advantage is not as valuable as unity of the people." The saying reflects the three fundamental dimensions of a problem the Chinese people take into consideration: time (opportunity), space (environment), and people. It reflects the basic notion of putting people at the center of everything.

引例 Citations：

◎天时、地利、人和，三者不得，虽胜有殃。（《孙膑兵法·月战》）
（有利的气候条件、有利的地理条件、人的齐心协力，这三者如不齐备，即便打了胜仗，自己也会蒙受损失。）

Favorable weather conditions, geographic advantages, and the unity of the people all must be in place. If not, even a victory won will be a very costly one. (*Sun Bin's Art of War*)

◎天时不如地利，地利不如人和。（《孟子·公孙丑下》）
（有利的气候条件不如有利的地理条件，有利的地理条件不如人的齐心协力。）

Favorable weather conditions are not as valuable as favorable geographic conditions, and favorable geographic conditions are not as valuable as the unity of the people. (*Mencius*)

tiānxià-wéigōng 天下为公

The World Belongs to All.

天下是公众的，天下为天下人所共有。"天下"，本义是"普天之下"，喻指君位、国家政权或整个国家，后泛指整个世界。"公"，大家、公众，狭义指贤人、德才兼备的人，广义指全体国民或天下所有的人。"天下为公"主要有两层意思：其一，君位非一人一姓所私有，而为有才德的人所共有，即所谓传贤不传子。其二，国家非一人一姓所私有，而为公众所共有。其中包含着反对君位世袭、主张推举有才德之人掌权的"尚贤"和"民本"思想。

古人相信,"天下为公"是实现"大同"社会、人民生活幸福的政治前提和保障。至近代,"天下为公"又演变成为推翻专制、实现民主的标志性关键词,后来成为一种美好的社会政治理想。

The world is a public realm and therefore belongs to all the people. *Tianxia* (天下), which literally means everything under heaven, used to refer to the monarch, state power, or the nation; later it extended to mean the whole world. In the narrow sense, *gong* (公) refers to figures with both integrity and competence, while in the broad sense it refers to all the people of a country, or everyone in the world. This term has two meanings. The first is that the position of a ruler is not the private property of just one person or his family, but rather belongs to all people of virtue and ability. Hence, the throne should be passed on to people according to their merit rather than through bloodline. The second meaning is that a country does not belong to a single individual or family, but belongs to the public. This is a people-centered vision, which opposes hereditary rule and believes that people with virtue and competence should be selected to exercise power. Ancient Chinese held this to be the foundation and guarantee for people to enjoy a happy life and realize universal harmony. In modern times, it evolved into a key concept calling for overthrowing autocracy and realizing democracy and later into a longing for an ideal society.

引例 Citation:

◎大道之行也,天下为公。选贤与能,讲信修睦。(《礼记·礼运》)
(大道实行的时代,天下为天下人所共有。品德高尚、才能突出的人被选拔出来管理社会,人与人之间讲求诚实与和睦。)

When the Great Way prevails, the world belongs to all the people. People of virtue and competence are chosen to govern the country; honesty is valued and people live in harmony. (*The Book of Rites*)

tiányuánshī 田园诗

Idyllic Poetry

　　一种以描写田园景色和田园生活为主要题材的诗歌流派。由东晋诗人陶渊明（365 或 372 或 376—427）开创。陶渊明的诗大部分取材于田园生活，语言质朴，画面平淡，但清新自然，意境深远，韵味醇厚。田园诗为中国古典诗歌开辟了一个新的境界，影响了六朝之后的诗歌发展。

A genre created by Tao Yuanming (365 or 372 or 376-427) of the Eastern Jin Dynasty, idyllic poetry depicts rural life and scenery. Taking country life as his favored theme, Tao Yuanming used plain language to portray rural scenes. His poems were unpretentious, refreshing, and natural, thus creating a far-reaching aesthetic conception and a lasting charm. Idyllic poetry represented a new stage in classical Chinese poetry and shaped poetic development in the Six Dynasties period and beyond.

引例 Citation：

◎以康乐之奥博，多溺于山水；以渊明之高古，偏放于田园。（白居易《与元九书》）

（谢灵运的诗深奥博大，但是多耽溺于山水；陶渊明的诗超拔古朴，却又多放情于田园。）

Xie Lingyun's poems are profound in implication, but focused excessively on mountain and water scenes, while Tao Yuanming's poems are graceful and simple, depicting mainly rural scenes. (Bai Juyi: Letter to Yuan Zhen)

wǎnyuēpài 婉约派

The *Wanyue* School / The Graceful and Restrained School

宋词两大流派之一。内容多写儿女之情、离别之绪，其特点是"专主情致"，表情达意讲究含蓄柔婉、隐约细腻，音律婉转谐和，语言圆润清丽。婉约词出现较早，名家辈出，唐五代有温庭筠（？—866）、李煜（937—978），宋初有柳永（987？—1053？）、晏殊（991—1055）、欧阳修（1007—1072）、晏几道（1038—1110），之后又有秦观（1049—1100）、贺铸（1052—1125）、周邦彦（1056—1121）、李清照（1084—1151？），南宋则有姜夔（1155？—1209）、吴文英（1212？—1272？）、张炎（1248—1314后）等一大批词人。在一千多年的词学发展中，婉约词风支配词坛，无论是数量还是质量，婉约派都占据主流和正统地位。需要说明的是，婉约派词人也抒写感时伤世之情，只是多将家国之恨、身世之感寓于抒情咏物，别有寄托，故不能一概以柔媚视之。

As one of the two *ci* (词) lyric schools of the Song Dynasty, the graceful and restrained school mainly dealt with romantic love or parting sorrow. It featured sentimental and nuanced expression of one's feelings, graceful and melodious metric patterning, and mellow and subtle use of language. *Ci* lyrics of this school emerged early, and many poets were famed for writing this style of *ci*, especially Wen Tingyun (?-866) and Li Yu (937-978) of the Five Dynasties period, Liu Yong (987?-1053?), Yan Shu (991-1055), Ouyang Xiu (1007-1072), Yan Jidao

(1038-1110), Qin Guan (1049-1100), He Zhu (1052-1125), Zhou Bangyan (1056-1121), and Li Qingzhao (1084-1151?) of the Northern Song Dynasty, as well as Jiang Kui (1155?-1209), Wu Wenying (1212?-1272?), and Zhang Yan (1248-1314?) of the Southern Song Dynasty. The graceful and restrained school occupied a dominant position in terms of both quantity and quality in over one thousand years of poetry's development. It should be mentioned that poets of this school also cared deeply about the fate of the nation, but they tended to express their concerns in a personal and sentimental way, often through depicting scenery. Therefore, their poems should not be regarded as lacking of vigor and energy.

引例 Citations：

◎至论其词，则有婉约者，有豪放者。婉约者欲其辞情蕴藉（jiè），豪放者欲其气象恢弘，盖虽各因其质，而词贵感人，要当以婉约为正。（徐师曾《文体明辨序说·诗余》）

（至于说到词，则有婉约风格的，有豪放风格的。婉约词其词句和情感追求含蓄而有意蕴，豪放词则追求气魄和境界宏大壮阔。这虽然是词作者的气质不同所致，但是词讲究以情动人，大体还是应该以婉约为正宗。）

Some *ci* lyrics are graceful and restrained, and some are bold and exuberant. The former are written in a nuanced way, whereas the latter are powerful and unrestrained. This difference is due to different temperament of poets. But *ci* lyrics are about expressing one's nuanced feelings, so the graceful and restrained school is representative of *ci* lyrics. (Xu Shizeng: *A Collection of Introductory Remarks on Various Styles*)

◎易安为婉约主，幼安为豪放主，此论非明代诸公所及。（沈曾（zēng）植《菌阁琐谈》）

（李清照是婉约词第一人，辛弃疾是豪放词第一人，这一见解明代诸位评论家并未提及。）

Li Qingzhao was the best *ci* poetess of the graceful and restrained school, whereas Xin Qiji was the best of the bold and unrestrained school. This view, important as it is, was not mentioned by literary critics of the Ming Dynasty. (Shen Zengzhi: *Random Notes on Ci Lyrics from Junge Studio*)

wángguózhīyīn 亡国之音

Music of a Failing State

　　国家将亡时的音乐，后多指颓靡荒淫的音乐。儒家认为，一个国家即将灭亡时，音乐多颓靡荒淫；而生活于社会底层的民众却困苦不堪，其音乐、诗歌等文艺作品一定充满了悲哀忧思。统治者若还不警醒，亡国也就为期不远了。

This term refers to the music of a state that is about to disintegrate. Later, it also refers to decadent and immoral music. The Confucian view was that music of a state on the verge of collapse tended to be dejected and demoralizing. As the downtrodden people endured immense suffering, their music and poetry were invariably full of sorrow and bitterness. If the ruler failed to wake up to the reality, the fall of his state was imminent.

引例 Citations：

◎亡国之音哀以思，其民困。(《礼记·乐记》)
（国家将亡时的音乐充满了悲哀忧思，这是因为民众困苦不堪的缘故。）

The music of a state on the verge of collapse reveals sorrow and anxiety because its people are in distress. (*The Book of Rites*)

◎郑卫之音，乱世之音也，比于慢矣。桑间濮上之音，亡国之音也。其政散，其民流，诬上行私而不可止也。(《礼记·乐记》)

（郑国和卫国的音乐，就是动乱时代的音乐，近乎轻慢无节制了。濮水岸边的桑间所流行的音乐，属于国家将亡时的音乐。它们反映出时政极端混乱，民众流离失所，臣下欺瞒君上、图谋私利而不可制止。）

The music of the states of Zheng and Wei was the music of an age of disorder, bordering on wantonness. The music of Sangjian on the Pushui River was typical of a failing state. The government was dysfunctional, the people were displaced, yet officials cheated on the ruler and pursued selfish gains with no one to stop them. (*The Book of Rites*)

wúwéi'érzhì 无为而治

Rule Through Non-action

不过度作为而把国家治理得很好。"治"指国家治理达到良好状态；"无为"不是不作为，而是不妄为。在道家那里，其要义在于顺其自然，即治国者充分尊重治理对象（民众）自身的禀性、状态和趋向，不过分干预民众的生活，使之遵循人自身固有的本性、意愿和逻辑，自我发展，自我实现，以无为而达到无不为，其哲学基础是"道法自然"。在儒家那里，其要义在于以德化民，即治国者不以政令、刑法等强加于人，而是从自身做起，以自身的道德和功业使民众受到影响和感化，使民众"不令而行"，实现天下大治，犹言"人文化成"。儒、道两家的共通点在于：治国者不妄加作为，不过度干预，充分尊重民众或社会的主体性。

Zhi (治) here means a state of good governance; *wuwei* (无为non-action) does not mean doing nothing, but instead not acting in an over-assertive manner, in other words, not imposing one's will. In Daoist thinking, this expression means the ruler must respect the natural conditions of those governed (the people); he must not interfere unduly in their lives but allow them to follow their own desires and ways to fulfill themselves. Through "non-action" everything will be actually achieved. The focus is "Dao operates naturally." In Confucian thinking, "non-action" means the ruler governs by influencing and motivating his subjects through his moral example and achievements, not through decrees, or coercive punishments, so that they act without being ordered, and social harmony is achieved. The focus here is something similar to "teaching people essential ideals and principles and guiding them to embrace goodness so as to build a harmonious social order." Both the Confucian and Daoist schools of thought advocate governance through respect for the intrinsic nature of people and society, not through too much interference or imposition.

引例 Citations：

◎道常无为而无不为。侯王若能守之，万物将自化。(《老子·三十七章》)
(道总是对万物不加干涉而成就万物。君主如果能够持守住它，万事万物就会自我生长。)

Dao always makes all things possible through non-interference with them. If the ruler can strictly follow this, then all things and creatures will grow of their own accord. (*Laozi*)

◎子曰："无为而治者，其舜也与（yú）！夫何为哉？恭己正南面而已矣。"
(《论语·卫灵公》)
(孔子说："能够无所作为而天下治理得很好的人，大概只有舜吧？他做了些什么呢？只是庄严端正地坐在天子之位上罢了。"）

Confucius said, "Who was the best at ruling through non-action? Probably Shun. And what did he do? Just sat solemnly upright on his imperial throne." (*The Analects*)

wùhuà 物化

Transformation of Things

事物彼我界限的打破及相互转化，是事物的一种存在状态。"物化"一说出自《庄子·齐物论》。庄子（前369？—前286）通过"庄周梦蝶"的寓言来说明"物化"的意义。庄子认为，自身与他者、梦与醒以及一切事物之间的界限与区别都可以被破除，从而实现物与物之间的转化与流通。如果执著于彼我的区别，就不能体认"物化"，如在梦中一般；但如果执著于"物化"，同样会跌入梦中。

This is a form of the existence of things when the boundary between things is broken and one thing transforms into another. The term "transformation of things" comes from *Zhuangzi,* in which the author Zhuangzi (369?-286 BC) illustrated the concept in the fable Zhuangzi Dreamed of Becoming a Butterfly. He believed that the boundary and difference between oneself and others, between in a dream and being awake, and between all things can be broken. Consequently, one may achieve the transformation between one thing and another. However, if one holds onto the difference between oneself and the others, one cannot achieve the transformation of things, as if in a dream. If one is bent on transforming things, one may still fall into a dream.

引例 Citation：

◎昔者庄周梦为胡蝶，栩栩然胡蝶也，自喻适志与（yú）！不知周也。俄然觉，则蘧（qú）蘧然周也。不知周之梦为胡蝶与？胡蝶之梦为周与？周与胡蝶，则必有分矣。此之谓物化。(《庄子·齐物论》)
（从前庄周梦见自己变成了蝴蝶，翩翩飞舞的一只蝴蝶，遨游各处悠游自在，不知道自己是庄周。忽然醒过来，自己分明是庄周。不知道是庄周做梦化为蝴蝶呢，还是蝴蝶做梦变化为庄周呢？庄周与蝴蝶必定是有所分别的。这就叫做"物化"。）

Once I, Zhuangzi, dreamed that I became a flying butterfly, happy with myself and doing as I pleased. I forgot that I was Zhuangzi. Suddenly I woke up and I was Zhuangzi again. I did not know whether Zhuangzi had been dreaming that he was a butterfly, or whether a butterfly had been dreaming that it was Zhuangzi. There must be a difference between the two, which is what I call the "transformation of things." (*Zhuangzi*)

xīkūn tǐ 西昆体

The Xikun Poetic Style

　　北宋初年出现的以追求辞藻华美、对仗工整为主要特征的诗歌流派。宋初，杨亿（974—1020）、刘筠（970—1030）、钱惟演（977—1034）等人聚集在皇帝藏书的秘阁（"西昆"代指皇帝藏书的地方），编纂历代君臣事迹，诏题《册府元龟》。他们在编书之余，写诗相互唱和，并结集为《西昆酬唱集》，时人因称之为"西昆体"。"西昆体"诗人提倡学习李商隐（813？—858？），讲求用典精巧、意旨幽深，重视音律与借代，其作品词采精丽、音节铿锵、属（zhǔ）对工整，一扫晚唐五代以后平直浅俗的诗风，在诗歌发展史上有一定影响。由于是酬唱之作，大都雕琢太过，缺乏真情实感，常流于艳浮，为后人诟病。

This poetic style pursued rhetorical beauty and symmetrical structure. In the early years of the Northern Song Dynasty, poets such as Yang Yi (974-1020), Liu Yun (970-1030), and Qian Weiyan (977-1034) gathered in the emperor's private library to compile *Important Mirrors for Governance*, a book that records the activities of monarchs and their ministers in all previous dynasties. During spare time, they wrote poems to each other. Later, they put these poems into a collection titled *A Collection of Xikun Poems*. (Xikun, in an ancient Chinese legend, was a place where books of emperors were supposedly housed, thus the title for their collected poems.) Xikun style poets drew inspiration from Li Shangyin (813?-858?), who was meticulous about the use of allusions and whose poems had subtle appeal. These poets prized metrical rigor and metonymy. Their works were exquisite in diction, highly rhythmical, and strictly parallel, doing away with the insipid and shallow features of poetic style in the late Tang as well as the following Five Dynasties and Ten States period. Xikun style poetry exerted a considerable influence on poetry writing in the later periods. However, being written impromptu just to echo each other, such poems tend to be overly polished and lacking in true sentiments, and their vanity was frowned upon by later critics.

引例 Citation：

◎ 盖自杨、刘唱和，《西昆集》行，后进学者争效之，风雅一变，谓之"昆体"。由是唐贤诸诗集几废而不行。（欧阳修《六一诗话》）

（大约自从杨亿、刘筠开始唱和，《西昆酬唱集》风行，后辈学人争相效仿，诗风为之改变，因而称之为"昆体"。从这以后，唐代诗人的诗集几乎被人遗忘而不流传了。）

After Yang Yi and Liu Yun wrote poems to each other, *A Collection of Xikun Poems* became popular, and its style was emulated by poets of the later periods, thus transforming the poetic style. A new way to write poetry, known as the Xikun style, emerged. From then on, collections of Tang poems were all but forgotten. (Ouyang Xiu: *Ouyang Xiu's Criticism of Poetry*)

xiāngyuàn 乡愿

Hypocrite

  以伪善的方式在乡里博取良好名声的人。"乡愿"之人只是在某些言行上表面合乎道义，以此博取世人的称誉，而实际上放弃原则和操守，谄媚于人，同流合污。"乡愿"貌似君子而实非君子，其言行表现，往往会混淆人们的道德判断，构成对社会道德的极大破坏。

A hypocrite is one who uses deceptive ways to seek a good local reputation. Hypocrites appear to behave in accordance with moral principles so as to win popular praise, while in reality compromising principles and personal integrity, currying favor, and colluding with dishonorable people. Hypocrites appear to be virtuous superior persons, but in reality are not. Their conduct often causes confusion in moral judgment, posing a tremendous threat to social morality.

引例 Citations：

◎子曰："乡原，德之贼也。"（《论语·阳货》）

（孔子说："乡愿，是道德的败坏者。"）

Confucius said, "A hypocrite is a moral degenerate." (*The Analects*)

◎阉然媚于世也者，是乡原也。(《孟子·尽心下》)

（曲意谄媚世人的人，就是乡愿。）

Those who please the world with hidden intentions are hypocrites. (*Mencius*)

xiào 孝

Filial Piety

　　子女对父母的顺从与敬爱。就言行而论，"孝"包含以下三点要求：其一，要谨慎保护受之于父母的身体，以免伤病，令父母担忧。其二，不能违背父母的教导、要求，即便不能认同，也应顺从遵循。其三，应以高尚的德行，成就自己的声誉与功业，以彰显父母的教导。"孝"植根于子女内心对父母的亲爱与尊敬。儒家认为，"孝"是个人德行养成的基础，并将其作为维系和强化父子关系乃至君臣关系的根本。

Filial piety is obedience to, and respect and love for your parents. To observe this, you must do the following. First, attentively keep your body, born by parents, safe from injury and illness so as to relieve them of their worries. Second, do not go against your parents' teachings, guidance and requests; obey them even if you do not agree with them. Third, gain fame and become accomplished through moral integrity, so as to highlight their teachings and guidance. Filial piety is rooted in children's love and respect for their parents. Confucians believe that filial piety is the foundation of a person's moral integrity and the basis for maintaining and strengthening the parent-child relationship, and even the sovereign-subject relationship.

引例 Citations：

◎子游问孝。子曰："今之孝者，是谓能养。至于犬马，皆能有养。不敬，何以别乎？"（《论语·为政》）

（子游请教什么是孝。孔子说："今日所谓的孝，是能奉养父母。对于犬、马，都能够饲养。如果不能尊敬父母，那么如何将奉养父母与饲养犬马相区别呢？"）

Ziyou asked Confucius about filial piety and Confucius replied, "Filial piety nowadays means taking care of your parents. But even dogs and horses can be taken care of; without respect, what is the difference between taking care of your parents and taking care of dogs and horses?" (*The Analects*)

◎夫孝，始于事亲，中于事君，终于立身。（《孝经·开宗明义》）

（孝，初始于服侍父母，发展为侍奉君主，归终于处事、为人之道。）

Filial piety starts with serving parents; it proceeds to serving the sovereign; it is completed by working and behaving within the rules of conduct. (*Classic of Filial Piety*)

xīnzhāi 心斋

Pure State of the Mind

心灵进入完全虚静的状态。出自《庄子·人间世》。书中借由孔子（前551—前479）之口向颜回（前521—前481）讲解"心斋"之义。庄子（前369？—前286）认为，耳和心在感知外物时，有彼我、是非之别。而气则虚无恬淡，处于万物之中而不与之分别、冲突。因此应使心变得如气一般虚

127

无，与外物相接触，却不与之分别、对立。心游离于事物之外，摆脱事物的限制与影响，这便是"心斋"。

The term refers to a state of mind that is completely empty and void. It originates from the book *Zhuangzi*, in which the meaning of the term was explained by Confucius (551-479 BC) to Yan Hui (521-481 BC). Zhuangzi (369?-286 BC) believed that one's ears and heart distinguish between oneself and others and between right and wrong, while *qi* (气 vital force), shapeless and empty, exists in everything and does not come into conflict with anything. Therefore, one's mind should be empty like *qi* when coming into contact with external things so that one will not be different or clash with them. When one's mind roams beyond physical things, freeing itself from the constraints and influence of other things, it maintains a state known as the "pure state of mind."

引例 Citation：

◎回曰："敢问心斋。"仲尼曰："若一志，无听之以耳而听之以心，无听之以心而听之以气。听止于耳，心止于符。气也者，虚而待物者也。唯道集虚，虚者心斋也。"(《庄子·人间世》)

(颜回说："请问什么是'心斋'？"孔子说："你心志专一，不用耳去听而用心去体悟，不用心去体悟而用气去感应。耳的作用止于聆听外物，心的作用止于应合事物。气乃是虚无而能容纳外物的。道只能集于虚无之气中，虚静的心灵就是'心斋'。")

Yan Hui said, "Could I ask what the 'pure state of the mind' means?" Confucius answered, "You should get totally focused. You need not listen with your ears but listen with your mind; you need not even listen with your mind but listen with *qi*. Listening stops at the ears, and the mind reaches only what fits it. *Qi* is empty and accommodates all external things. Dao gathers and presents itself in an unoccupied and peaceful mind; being unoccupied means the pure state of the mind." (*Zhuangzi*)

xíngjǐ-yǒuchǐ 行己有耻

Conduct Oneself with a Sense of Shame

对自己的言行保持羞耻之心。出自《论语》。在孔子（前551—前479）看来，一个人的德行的养成不只是言语、行为符合外在的规范，更要在内心对于自身的不足或违礼背德之行感到羞耻，进而能够在羞耻心的刺激下，按照德礼的要求改正、完善自己的言行。羞耻心的确立是儒家教化的重要目标。

The term is from *The Analects*. From the point of view of Confucius (551-479 BC), the cultivation of moral conduct is not only words and deeds in accordance with social norms, but more importantly one should have a sense of shame about personal inadequacies and violations of moral conduct. Moreover, stimulated by a sense of shame, one can correct and perfect self-conduct in accordance with moral and social norms. The establishment of a sense of shame is an important goal of Confucian teaching.

引例 Citations：

◎子贡问曰："何如斯可谓之士矣？"子曰："行己有耻，使于四方，不辱君命，可谓士矣。"(《论语·子路》)

（子贡请教："如何做才可以称为士？"孔子说："对自己的言行保持羞耻之心，出使四方诸侯，不辱没君主赋予的使命，就可以称为士了。"）

Zigong asked, "What qualifies a person to be called a *shi* (roughly referring to those at the social stratum between the aristocracy and the common people)?" Confucius said, "He who conducts himself with a sense of shame, and does not disgrace the tasks entrusted by his sovereign when dispatched elsewhere, may be called a *shi*." (*The Analects*)

◎子曰:"道(dǎo)之以政,齐之以刑,民免而无耻。道之以德,齐之以礼,有耻且格。"(《论语·为政》)

(孔子说:"用政令加以引导,用刑罚加以规范,民众能免于罪过,但没有羞耻之心。用道德加以引导,用礼义加以规范,民众不但有羞耻之心,而且能够自觉合于规范。")

Confucius said, "If people are guided by governmental decree and made to behave themselves through punishments, they will avoid punishment, but will have no sense of shame. If they are guided by morality and behave themselves in accordance with social norms, they will have a sense of shame and will follow rules." (*The Analects*)

xìng'è 性恶

Human Nature Is Evil.

荀子(前313?—前238)提出的一种人性论观点。荀子所言人性,指人天生所具有的属性,包括身体的生命特征及各种欲望、知觉等。如果仅仅因循于人性中所包含的对外物的欲求,就会导致人与人之间的纷争,社会将陷入混乱。而维系社会秩序所必需的道德,并非出自人的本性,而是后天人为塑造的结果。

This view was proposed by Xunzi (313?-238 BC). According to him, human nature, which refers to proprieties humans naturally possess, includes physical life as well as various desires and perceptions. If people are allowed to only follow desire for external things, which is something inherent in human nature, it will lead to conflicts, and the society will fall into chaos. Moral conduct which is vital for maintaining order in society does not derive from human nature. Rather, it is acquired through deliberate efforts.

引例 Citations：

◎人之性恶，其善者伪也。(《荀子·性恶》)

（人的本性中只具有为恶的成分，人的善行都是后天人为的。）

Human nature is evil, while a good conduct is always acquired. (*Xunzi*)

◎今人之性恶，必将待师法然后正，得礼义然后治。(《荀子·性恶》)

（今人的本性中只具有为恶的成分，必须要依赖师长的教化而后才能端正，有礼义的约束而后才能安定。）

As human nature is evil, it must be corrected with moral teaching. Human nature can only be reined in with rites and righteousness. (*Xunzi*)

xìngshàn 性善

Human Nature Is Good.

孟子（前372？—前289）提出的一种人性论观点。孟子所言人性，指人天生所具有的人之所以为人的本质属性，亦即是人区别于禽兽的道德本性。这个意义上的人性，构成了仁、义、礼、智等德行的内在根基或依据。

但是，人性中具备的只是德行的端始，并不等于德行的实现或完成。人们需要不断扩充人性中的善端，才能确立起良好的德行。

This view on human nature was first proposed by Mencius. As Mencius (372?-289 BC) saw it, human nature is the inherent moral character which a human being naturally possesses and which distinguishes him from an animal. In this sense, human nature underpins such virtues as benevolence, righteousness, sound social norms, and good judgment. However, good human nature does not automatically constitute virtuous conduct. People need to continuously cultivate good human nature in order to develop virtuous conduct.

引例 Citations：

◎孟子道性善，言必称尧、舜。(《孟子·滕文公上》)

（孟子讲述性善之说，言谈必称述尧、舜的事迹。）

When Mencius spoke about human nature being good, he always referred to the exploits of Emperor Yao and Emperor Shun. (*Mencius*)

◎孟子有大功于世，以其言性善也。（朱熹《孟子序说》引程子语）

（孟子对于世间有着卓越的功绩，是因为他提出了性善之说。）

Mencius made a great contribution to the world by proposing that human nature is good. (Chengzi, as quoted in Zhu Xi: An Introduction to *Mencius Variorum*)

xuányánshī 玄言诗

Metaphysical Poetry

一种以阐发老庄、佛教和《周易》哲理为主要内容的诗歌流派，起于西晋末年而盛行于东晋，其主要特点是以玄理入诗，代表诗人有孙绰（314—371）、许询（314—361）、庾亮（289—340）、桓温（312—373）等。魏晋时期社会动荡，士大夫专心老庄与佛学，贵玄理，尚清谈，以此全身远祸。到西晋后期，玄谈之风逐步影响到诗歌创作，形成玄言诗，后玄言诗与山水诗相融合。

This term refers to a poetic style that chiefly explicated Laozi, Zhuangzi (369?-286 BC), Buddhism, and *The Book of Changes*. Metaphysical poetry emerged at the end of the Western Jin Dynasty and flourished during the subsequent Eastern Jin Dynasty. Represented by Sun Chuo (314-371), Xu Xun (314-361), Yu Liang (289-340), and Huan Wen (312-373), this genre featured the expounding of abstruse and metaphysical thinking in poetry. During the turbulent years of the Wei and Jin dynasties, scholars stayed away from politics and focused on the study of Laozi, Zhuangzi, and Buddhism to explore abstruse and philosophical ideas unrelated to current social developments. By the end of the Western Jin Dynasty, this rarefied discourse found its way into writing, creating the metaphysical style of poetry, which later merged with landscape poetry.

引例 Citation：

◎自中朝贵玄，江左称盛，因谈余气，流成文体，是以世极迍邅（zhūnzhān），而辞意夷泰。诗必柱下之旨归，赋乃漆园之义疏。（刘勰《文心雕龙·时序》）

（自从西晋崇尚玄学，到东晋风气更盛，因袭清谈风气，逐渐形成新的文风。因此，虽然时势极其艰难，而文章的辞意却显得平和宽缓。诗歌必定以老庄为宗旨，辞赋也成了老庄的注解。）

In the Western Jin Dynasty, discourse of metaphysics was hot, which became even more popular during the Eastern Jin Dynasty, giving rise to a new literary style. Consequently, despite the tumultuous times, writers composed literary works characterized by detachment and aloofness. Poetry invariably illustrated the ideas of Laozi and Zhuangzi, and prose-poetry became commentaries on these two thinkers. (Liu Xie: *The Literary Mind and the Carving of Dragons*)

《Xuǎn》tǐ, xuǎntǐ 选体

Xuanti Poetry / Poetry in Prince Zhaoming's Favorite Style

主要指南朝梁昭明太子萧统（501—531）《文选》中所收汉魏以来的五言古诗。但这一概念后来超越了单纯的诗歌体式而兼具时代特征与诗歌风格等含义。在体式上，"选体"是与乐府、歌行、律绝并列的概念，在古人眼光中，它几乎就是五言古诗的代名词，是诗家创作五古的范式；在风格上，"选体"有典雅、翰藻、新创三个主要特征；从时代看，"选体"接续风骚，历跨汉魏、晋宋、齐梁。唐代以后，文论家多用"选体"这一术语来评诗、论诗。但"选体"派强调模仿古人，为此受到后来一些锐意创新的文人的批评。

This refers mainly to the five-character-a-line poems of the Han and Wei dynasties in *Selections of Refined Literature* compiled by Xiao Tong (501-531), Crown Prince Zhaoming of the Liang Dynasty during the Southern Dynasties.

Later, this term meant not just a specific type of poetry, but also both the prevailing poetic features of an era and general poetic style. Poems of this style were regarded as in the same rank as *yuefu* (乐府) poetry, which were folk songs and ballads collected and compiled by the Han government office in charge of musical preservation, or any poetic imitation equally suitable for musical composition, as well as *gexing* (歌行), which were odes to events or physical objects in free-verse form, and *lüjüe* (律绝), or poetry with fixed patterns. To poetic critics in later generations, *xuanti* (选体) poetry was synonymous with five-character poetry and was a standard way to write poems with five characters per line. In terms of style, it is elegant, richly colorful, and innovative. This type of poetry inherited the poetic tradition all the way from *The Book of Songs* and *Odes of Chu* to the Han and Wei dynasties, the Jin Dynasty, and the Song, Qi, and Liang during the Southern Dynasties. From the Tang Dynasty onward, many literary critics used the term "*xuanti* poetry" as a standard in their comments on poetry. This poetic style was criticized later by some creative-minded poets for its excessive emphasis on following the classical tradition.

引例 Citations：

◎五言诗，三百五篇中间（jiàn）有之，逮汉魏苏、李、曹、刘之作，号为"《选》体"。(刘克庄《林子䍧（xiǎn）》)

（五言诗在《诗经》中只是间或出现，到汉魏时期苏武、李陵、曹操、刘桢等人的创作[才得以定形，又因《文选》收录，故而]被称为"《文选》体"。）

Five-character-a-line poems were found occasionally in *The Book of Songs*. By the Han and Wei dynasties, Su Wu, Li Ling, Cao Cao, and Liu Zhen had written more five-character-a-line poems and established the style. These poems were collected in *Selections of Refined Literature* and therefore the style is known as the *xuanti* style. (Liu Kezhuang: Preface to *A Collection of Poems by Lin Zixian*)

◎昭明选古诗，人遂以其所选者为"古诗"，因而名古诗曰"选体"。唐人之古诗曰"唐选"。呜呼！非惟古诗亡，几并古诗之名而亡之矣。（钟惺《诗归·序》）

（昭明太子选古诗，后人于是把他所选的诗称为古诗，因此就称古诗为"选体"。唐代人创作的古诗叫做"唐选"。可惜啊！不仅古诗消亡了，就连"古诗"这一名称也跟着消亡了。）

Prince Zhaoming selected ancient poems, which people of later generations would call "ancient poems." They were also known as *xuanti* poetry or poetry in Prince Zhaoming's favorite style. The works by Tang-dynasty poets were called Tang *xuanti* poetry. But now, alas, ancient poetry has become extinct; even the term itself is sadly forgotten. (Zhong Xing: Preface to *The Purport of Poetic Creation*)

yífēng-yìsú 移风易俗

Change Social Practices and Customs

转移风气，改变习俗。"移风易俗"是"乐"的重要功能。风俗是社会群体长期以来形成的共同的行为习惯，可能会包含某些违礼的成分。群体习惯的改变十分困难，不能单纯依赖强制的规范，而是需要发挥"乐"对于人心的深刻影响。通过"乐"的教化，引导人心进入恰当的状态，进而逐渐改变社会的风气和习俗，使之自觉符合礼的要求。

This is one of the important functions of music. Social practices are common forms of behavior formed within communities over time, and they can also include aspects that do not conform to rites. Changing such widespread habits is extremely difficult and cannot be accomplished by mandatory regulations alone. This is where music comes into play by affecting and stirring people's emotions so that they gradually change their ways and willingly conform to the requirements of rites.

引例 Citation：

◎乐者，圣人之所乐（lè）也，而可以善民心，其感人深，其移风易俗，故先王导之以礼乐而民和睦。(《荀子·乐论》)
（"乐"是圣人所喜好的，可以使百姓之心向善，对人有极强的感染力，能移风易俗，因此先王用礼乐引导民众，使他们和睦相处。）

Music was appreciated by the sages; it improves people's behavior, stirs and moves them, so they change social practices and customs. Thus the sage kings guided their subjects with music and rites, so that the subjects treated each other with friendship and good will. (*Xunzi*)

yǐzhàn-zhǐzhàn 以战止战

Use War to Stop War

用战争制止战争。这是中华民族自古秉持的一种战争观。前一个"战"是指正义的战争；后一个"战"是指非正义的战争。正义的战争是反抗强加在自己头上的非正义战争而不得已采取的行动，其目的是除暴安良、护国保民，制止并最终消灭非正义战争，实现人类和平，使广大民众过上幸福安宁的生活。它表现了中华民族崇尚正义、爱好和平的"文"的精神，与"止戈为武"异曲同工。

This is an ancient Chinese belief on the role of war. The first "war" means a just war, the second an unjust one. A just war is waged to resist a war that has been forced upon one. It is not of one's choosing, but is fought to defend the country and the people from imposed violence, in order to ultimately end the war and restore peace and stability. It expresses the "civil" spirit of the Chinese nation that believes in justice and peace. It is similar in meaning to "stopping war is a true craft of war."

引例 Citations：

◎夫武，禁暴、戢兵、保大、定功、安民、和众、丰财者也。(《左传·宣公十二年》)

(武功是用来禁止强暴、消除战争、保持强大、巩固功业、安定百姓、调和大众、丰富财物的。)

The purpose of military action should include the following seven tasks: to prohibit violence, stop wars, maintain one's strength, safeguard achievements, give peace to the people, bring harmony to the multitudes, and enrich the state's resources. (*Zuo's Commentary on The Spring and Autumn Annals*)

◎古者，以仁为本、以义治之之谓正。……是故杀人安人，杀之可也；攻其国，爱其民，攻之可也；以战止战，虽战可也。(《司马法·仁本》)

(古人以仁爱为根本、以治军是否合乎道义称之为正道。……所以，如果杀掉坏人是为了使大众得到安宁，杀人是可以的；如果进攻别的国家是出于爱护它的民众，进攻是可以的；如果能用战争制止战争，进行战争也是可以的。)

The ancient people considered benevolent love to be the foundation of society, and the use of force in ethical ways as the proper way… If getting rid of the wicked is for the common good, then killing is permissible; if attacking another country is to protect its people, the attack is well-founded; if war is used to stop war, then it is justified. (*The General Commander's Treatise on War*)

yǐnyìshī 隐逸诗

Recluse Poetry

指归隐山林、田园的文人，以山林、田园生活为创作题材并寄寓个人志趣情怀的诗歌。古代有些文人，因不屑于做官或对当时的社会政治不满，转而归隐山林、田园，成为隐士。他们常常借描摹山水、田园等自然景物来表达高蹈遗世的精神旨趣。其中，陶渊明（365 或 372 或 376—427）被称为"古今隐逸诗人之宗"。唐宋以后，很多文人士大夫从陶渊明的生活方式中受到启发，在山林、田园生活中寻求心灵安顿，于是产生了有隐逸倾向的诗歌作品。

Recluse poetry refers to poems written by literary figures who retreated to the remote mountains or countryside and expressed their sentiments through depicting this kind of life. Some Chinese scholars in the old days, having disdain for taking official position or were dissatisfied with political reality of the day, chose to live in seclusion in mountains and forests or in the countryside. They expressed their pursuit of a state of mind that transcended the worldly through depicting images of mountains, rivers, and other natural scenes. Tao Yuanming (365 or 372 or 376-427) is regarded as the forerunner of this genre. Inspired by his recluse lifestyle, many learned men in the post-Tang and Song period also sought solace and peace of mind in the mountains and countryside, thus giving rise to recluse poetry.

引例 Citation：

◎其源出于应璩（qú），又协左思风力。文体省净，殆无长（zhàng）语。笃意真古，辞兴婉惬。每观其文，想其人德……古今隐逸诗人之宗也。（钟嵘《诗品》卷中）

（[陶诗]源于应璩，又兼有左思的风骨。陶诗简洁纯净，基本没有什么多余的词句。诗人致力于传达真淳古朴的观念，文词用兴寄手法而委婉恰切。每每读到他的诗文，都会想起他的形貌和品德……真是古今隐逸诗人中的第一人啊！）

While inspired by Ying Qu's work, Tao Yuanming's poems also inherited Zuo Si's powerful expression. His style is simple and lucid, and there are no redundant words in his poems. He devoted himself to expressing simple and unsophisticated ideas by means of association in mild, appropriate language. When we read his works, we see in them a man with noble character… He was truly the most distinguished of the recluse poets ever produced! (Zhong Rong: *The Critique of Poetry*)

Yǒngmíng tǐ 永明体

The Yongming Poetic Style

南朝齐武帝永明年间（483—493）出现的、以讲求声韵对偶为主要特征的诗歌风格。也称"新体诗"（与汉魏以来的"古体诗"相对而言）。代表人物是谢朓（tiǎo，464—499）、沈约（441—513）和王融（467—493）。"永明体"标志着诗人已经熟练掌握声韵对偶的规律并自觉运用于诗歌创作，增加了诗歌的形式美感与艺术表现力，为近体诗的产生奠定了基础。不足的是，"永明体"过于受声韵拘束，内容有所削弱，受到当时一些诗论家的批评，在新变中也蕴藏了危机。

Poems of this style first emerged during the reign of Emperor Wu of Qi of the Southern Dynasties. That period, lasting from 483 to 493, assumed the regal title of Yongming, hence the name of this poetic style. Yongming poems featured metrical structure and parallelism. They were also known as the "new poetry," as opposed to the "old poetry" of the Han Dynasty and the Wei period. Xie Tiao (464-499), Shen Yue (441-513), and Wang Rong (467-493) were leading poets of the Yongming style. This style was marked by a poet's deft use of metrical structure and parallelism, thus enhancing the stylistic beauty and artistic expressiveness of poetry. It laid the foundation for the emergence of the "early modern" poetry, or regulated verse. However, the Yongming poetic style was weakened by an excessive emphasis on tonal patterns at the cost of content, drawing criticism of some poetry critics of the time. The style was thus burdened by this inherent risk in its quest for innovation.

引例 Citation：

◎永明末，盛为文章，吴兴沈约、陈郡谢朓、琅琊王融以气类相推毂，汝南周颙（yóng）善识声韵。约等文皆用宫商，以平上去入为四声，以此制韵，不可增减，世呼为"永明体"。（《南齐书·陆厥传》）

（永明末年，文学创作大盛，吴兴人沈约、陈郡人谢朓、琅琊人王融等以共同的志趣相互推举，汝南人周颙精通声韵。沈约等人的创作都讲求音律，以平声、上声、去声、入声为四声，以此来创制韵律，不能随意增加或减少，世人称之为"永明体"。）

Literary writing flourished towards the end of the Yongming period. Shen Yue from Wuxing, Xie Tiao from Chenjun, and Wang Rong from Langya, encouraged and praised each other out of their shared artistic aspirations. Zhou Yong from Runan was well versed in metrical patterning. The poems by Shen Yue and the others were very strict about the use of metrical schemes, namely, the level tone, the rising tone, the falling-rising tone, and the falling tone, and departure from the strict use of such metrical schemes was forbidden. This particular style of poetic creation became known as the Yongming style. (*The History of Qi of the Southern Dynasties*)

yǒngshǐshī 咏史诗

Poetry on History

以历史事件或历史人物等作为创作题材并借以抒写诗人情志、感悟的诗歌。史实、史识与史情紧密结合是其主要特点。咏史诗多以"述古""怀古""览古""感古""古兴""读史""咏史"等为题，也有直接以被描写的历史人物、历史事件为标题的。

Poetry on history refers to poems written to convey a poet's sentiments by reflecting on historical events or historical figures. A poem on history touched on historical events and expressed the poet's historical insight as well as his emotional attachment to history. Such poems recounted, relived, revived, interpreted, or chanted about history. Some poets used historical figures or events as titles for such poems.

引例 Citation：

◎怀古者，见古迹，思古人其事。无他，兴亡贤愚而已。（方回《瀛奎律髓》卷三）

(怀古之作，是诗人见到古迹，于是追思古人的往事。不为别的，不过是抒写对历史兴亡和古人贤愚的看法与感悟罢了。)

Poems on history are written when poets see historical sites that take their minds to the past. In these poems, poets reflect on the rise and fall of past dynasties as well as the wisdom and folly of historical figures. (Fang Hui: *The Best Regulated Poems of the Tang and Song Dynasties*)

yuánhēng-lìzhēn, yuán-hēng-lì-zhēn 元亨利贞

Yuanheng Lizhen

《周易·乾卦》的卦辞。主要有两种理解：其一，从占筮的角度来看，"元亨，利贞"是依据所得之卦来预测吉凶的断语。"元亨"意为大通，或举行大享的祭礼。"利贞"指利于占问，即筮得此卦为吉。其二，从义理的角度来看，"元亨利贞"被认为是乾卦的四种品德。有人将四者对应为仁、礼、义、正，又有人将其作为万物从始生到成熟的四个阶段，或指天道、圣人生养万物的四种德行。

This is a term used in *The Book of Changes* to explain the meaning of hexagrams. It may be understood in two ways. First, when used in divination, it is a judgment predicting good fortune. *Yuanheng* (元亨) means a wide, smooth path or a grand sacrificial rite. *Lizhen* (利贞) refers to a favorable reading by a diviner and an auspicious prospect. Second, from the point of view of morality, it is believed to stand for four virtues associated with the *qian* (乾) hexagram. One view is that the four virtues are benevolence, rites, righteousness, and integrity; other views are that they represent four stages of life from birth to maturity, or four forms of moral conduct dictated by the way of heaven and adhered to by the sage in caring for all creatures.

引例 Citations:

◎君子体仁，足以长人；嘉会，足以合礼；利物，足以和义；贞固，足以干事。君子行此四德者，故曰"乾，元亨利贞。"（《周易·文言》）
（君子体会仁德，足以成为人们的尊长；将美好之物汇聚，足以合于礼；使万物得利，足以符合义；端正持守，足以成事。君子奉行这四种德行，因此称"乾，元亨利贞"。）

A man of virtue, embodying benevolence, is able to preside over others. Bringing together everything good, he is able to conform with the rites. Bringing benefits to all, he is able to conform with righteousness. Being steadfast and firm, he is able to manage affairs. A man of virtue acts in accordance with these four virtues, and hence it is said: *Qian* is *yuan* (primal) and *heng* (prosperous), *li* (beneficial) and *zhen* (steadfast). (*The Book of Changes*)

◎元者万物之始，亨者万物之长，利者万物之遂，贞者万物之成。（程颐《程氏易传》卷一）
（"元"是万物的起始，"亨"是万物的生长，"利"是万物的发展，"贞"是万物的最终形成。）

Yuan symbolizes the beginning of all things, *heng* their growth, *li* their further development, and *zhen* their maturity. (Cheng Yi: *Cheng Yi's Commentary on The Book of Changes*)

yuàncì 怨刺

Resentment and Sting

用文学形式表达对社会不公的不满及对统治者的讽刺劝谏。特指《诗经》中对时政和统治者进行批判和讽喻，表达诗人心中强烈怨愤与不平的诗作。汉代学者认为《诗经》中的"怨"是有节制的宣泄，"刺"则是积极意义上的规劝，因此将二者合成一个文学批评术语，肯定这类作品所具有的现实意义。唐宋以后，此术语有激烈批判和强烈怨恨的意味，不过核心内涵仍以向往政治清明、社会和谐为旨归。

This term means using a literary form to express resentment towards social injustice and satirize and admonish those in power. It especially refers to the poems in *The Book of Songs*, in which poets criticized and satirized the politics and the ruling class of the time to vent their indignation and resentment. Scholars in the Han Dynasty considered resentment in *The Book of Songs* as controlled venting and the satiric sting constructive admonishment. They therefore combined the two into a term of literary criticism with positive implication. After the Tang and Song dynasties, the term gained a connotation of intense criticism and indignation. However, the essential meaning was still a yearning for good governance and social harmony.

引例 Citation：

◎周道始缺，怨刺之诗起。王泽既竭，而诗不能作。(《汉书·礼乐志》)
(在周代仁义之道遭到破坏之后，开始出现表达不满之情和讽劝之意的诗歌。当帝王对百姓的恩德完全失去之后，人们就不再用诗歌表达心声了。)

When the benevolent way of ruling in the Zhou Dynasty was abandoned, there appeared poems that expressed resentment towards those in power and satirized or admonished them. When the king no longer cared for the general public, people stopped using poems to express what they had in mind. (*The History of the Han Dynasty*)

yuēdìng-súchéng 约定俗成

Established Through Popular Usage / Accepted Through Common Practice

名称按约定确立并成为习惯。荀子（前 313？—前 238）提出"约定俗成"的观念，用以描述事物的命名方式。荀子认为，人们所使用的名称有着不同的种类，每个名称适用于指示特定的对象。但具体用哪个名称来指示某一事物或某类事物，则是由人们共同约定的。约定的名称用法逐渐为人们所习惯，那么这一名称也就确定下来了。"约定俗成"后来也被用以泛指一般社会规则的形成。

Names are established through popular usage. Xunzi (313?-238 BC) proposed this idea to describe how things are named. Xunzi believed that names fall into different categories, and every name is used to indicate a particular object. Which name is used to describe what or what kind of things is decided by the popularity of its use. When everybody accepts a name established by popular usage, it has become a fixed name for the particular object. This idea has also been used to describe the establishment of social norms.

引例 Citation：

◎名无固宜，约之以命。约定俗成谓之宜，异于约则谓之不宜。名无固实，

约之以命实，约定俗成谓之实名。(《荀子·正名》)
（名称没有本来就合适的，而是由人们约定而加以命名的。按照约定确立并为人们所习惯的名称就是适宜的，有别于约定的名称则称之为不适宜的。名称没有本来就指称某一对象，而是按照约定去指称特定的对象，名称按约定确立并成为习惯，就称之为某一对象的名称。）

There is no such thing as a name matches an object from the very beginning. All things are named in accordance with the popularity of their use by people. When everybody accepts a name, it is proper for the thing it refers to. Names that are not accepted or commonly used are not appropriate. Names are not originally meant to refer to a particular object; it is through popular use that a name comes to designate a particular thing. Once accepted through popular usage, a name has established its fixed association with the object it refers to. (*Xunzi*)

yuè 乐

Yue (Music)

古代六艺之一，常与"礼"并称。相较于各种外在的礼法规范，音乐最能感动人的内心并对人的言行产生影响。但并不是所有的音乐都属于儒家所说的"乐"的范畴。"乐"应能有助于人的性情处于平和中正的状态，使人的言行自觉符合礼的要求，从而实现人与人之间的和谐共处。"乐"常与其他礼仪形式配合运用，是维系人伦秩序、移风易俗的重要手段。

Yue (乐) is one of the six arts of ancient times, often mentioned together with *li* (礼 rites / social norms). In contrast to external rules and rites, music touches the emotions and thus can affect human behavior. However, not all music counts as the Confucian *yue* which must have the effect of making the listener calm and measured so as to willingly behave in accordance with social norms, and thus engage harmoniously with others. *Yue* is often associated with other forms of ceremonial actions; it is one important way of maintaining proper human relations and encouraging better social practices and customs.

引例 Citations：

◎乐也者，和之不可变者也；礼也者，理之不可易者也。乐合同，礼别异。礼乐之统，管乎人心矣。(《荀子·乐论》)

（没有一种东西能替代乐来促成社会的和谐，也没有一种东西能替代礼来分别社会的伦理差等。乐使人们相互和谐，礼使人们分别差等。礼和乐一起管控人心的各个方面。）

Nothing can replace music for creating social harmony, and nothing can replace rites for determining ethical social differences. Music brings people together in harmony; rites establish roles and relationships. Together they direct human morality. (*Xunzi*)

◎子曰："恶紫之夺朱也，恶郑声之乱雅乐也，恶利口之覆邦家者。"(《论语·阳货》)

（孔子说："我厌恶用紫色取代红色，厌恶用郑国的音乐扰乱雅正的音乐，憎恶伶牙俐齿而使国家倾覆的人。"）

Confucius said, "I detest replacing red with purple and interfering refined classical music with the music of the State of Zheng. I loathe those who overthrow the state with their glib tongues." (*The Analects*)

zhèngguìyǒuhéng 政贵有恒

Stability Is the Key to Governance.

国家大政贵在稳定持久。"政"指国家根本性的制度、法令、政策;"贵"即崇尚;"有恒"即保持稳定。一个国家,尤其是大国,一定要保持其根本制度、根本大法的稳定性、持久性,不能朝令夕改,反复无常,否则会引起政局动荡、社会混乱;尤其在根本性问题上不能出现颠覆性变化,否则难以挽回和弥补。这个道理和"治大国若烹小鲜"有相通之处。

It's the key to governance to ensure sustained stability. *Zheng* (政) refers to the fundamental systems, laws, and policies of a state. *Gui* (贵) means the most valuable thing. *Youheng* (有恒) means to ensure stability. A country, especially a large country, must preserve the constancy of its basic systems and fundamental laws. Laws, especially fundamental ones, must not be changed from time to time at random. Otherwise, the country will land into political turmoil and social chaos, resulting in irreversible and irreparable damages. This is the same notion as embodied in the saying "governing a big country is like cooking small fish."

引例 Citation:

◎政贵有恒,辞尚体要,不惟好异。(《尚书·毕命》)
(国家的大政贵在稳定持久,文辞贵在切实简要,不能一味追求标新立异。)

What is most valuable for governance lies in its sustained stability, advocating clear and straight wording, not seeking novelty. (*The Book of History*)

Zhèngshǐ tǐ 正始体

The Zhengshi Literary Style

指三国曹魏后期的文学风格。因始于魏齐王曹芳（232—274）正始（240—249）年间，故名。这一时期的政治现实极其严酷，正始文人因此以哲学眼光来看待、思考更为广阔的人生和宇宙问题。深刻的理性思考和强烈的人生悲哀，构成了正始文学最基本的特点。正始文学的主要特征是崇尚老庄，以玄理入诗，呈现出浓厚的哲理色彩。当时作家主要有两派：一派是以何晏（？—249）、王弼（226—249）为代表，开两晋"玄言诗"之先河；另一派是以嵇康（223—262，或 224—263）、阮籍（210—263）为代表，继承建安文学传统，其作品有深厚的思想感情、鲜明的时代特色和个性特点，因而成就较大。

The term refers to the literary style of the final years of the State of Wei in the Three Kingdoms period. It emerged in the Zhengshi era (240–249) under the reign of Cao Fang (232-274), also known as Prince Qi of Wei. Facing the harsh prevailing political conditions, literary figures of the era viewed life and the world in a broader and philosophical context, and profound and rational analysis as well as penetrating depiction of human tragedies were underlying features of their writings. Reverence for Laozi and Zhuangzi was a key feature of this literary style, with poetry, in particular, being abstruse and philosophical in terms of message. The Zhengshi style had two schools. One was represented by He Yan (?-249) and Wang Bi (226-249), whose works heralded the Jin-dynasty metaphysical poetry. The other school, represented by literary figures like Ji Kang (223-262 or 224-263) and Ruan Ji (210-263), was more influential.

Building on the Jian'an literary tradition, they conveyed in their writings profound thought and emotions, and gave vivid expression to social life at the time with intense individual characteristics.

引例 Citation：

◎ 及正始明道，诗杂仙心，何晏之徒，率多浮浅。唯嵇志清峻，阮旨遥深，故能标焉。（刘勰《文心雕龙·明诗》）
（到了正始年间，盛行道家思想，诗歌夹杂出尘求仙的内容。何晏等人的作品大都比较浅薄。只有嵇康的诗有清远高峻的情志，阮籍的诗表现出深远意旨，所以他们能高出同时代人。）

By the Zhengshi era, Daoism was popular and, as a result, poetry reflected people's desire to reach the immortal world. Works by He Yan and his followers were for the most part superficial. Only Ji Kang expressed lofty ideals, and Ruan Ji showed depth and insight in his poetry; they thus stood out among the writers of that age. (Liu Xie: *The Literary Mind and the Carving of Dragons*)

zhìnèi-cáiwài 治内裁外

Handling Internal Affairs Takes Precedence over External Affairs.

治理好国家的内部事务，才能处理好对外事务。"治内"是指国家内部的治理达到理想状态；"裁外"是指量度天下大势，制定对外政策，选择适当的政治、外交、军事等手段，影响国际格局。它告诉我们一条原理：国家内政是对外方略的基础。

A country's internal affairs must be handled well before its external affairs can be handled well. *Zhinei* (治内) means that domestic governance has achieved an ideal state; *caiwai* (裁外) means assessing the broad trends in the world, making external policies, and selecting appropriate political, diplomatic, and military measures to influence the international situation. This tells us a basic principle: a country's internal governance is the foundation of its external strategy.

引例 Citations：

◎内政不修，外举事不济。(《管子·大匡》)
（国内政务不去整治好，对外用兵就不会成功。）

If internal affairs are not handled properly, using military force externally will not succeed. (*Guanzi*)

◎三王不务离合而正，五霸不待从横（zònghéng）而察，治内以裁外而已矣。(《韩非子·忠孝》)
（夏、商、周三代开国君主没有致力于与谁疏远、与谁联合就能匡正天下，春秋五霸也没有搞合纵连横就能明察天下大势，他们不过是在治理好内政基础上再处理对外事务罢了。）

The founding rulers of the Xia, Shang, and Zhou dynasties did not try to impose order on the land by keeping their distance from some or becoming close to others, nor did the Five Most Powerful Kings of the Spring and Autumn Period discern the broad trends in the world by forming vertical or horizontal alliances. They managed external affairs only after they had handled their internal affairs well. (*Hanfeizi*)

zhìshìzhīyīn 治世之音

Music of an Age of Good Order

指太平时代的音乐。儒家认为，音乐与社会政治相互联通，音乐能反映一个国家的政治盛衰得失及社会风俗的变化。乐教能促使政治清明，社会秩序稳定；反过来，太平时代政治开明、和美，其音乐、诗歌作品一定充满祥和欢乐。"治世之音"也被用来指《诗经》中的某些美颂之作。

Confucian scholars believed that music interacts with both society and its political evolution; it also reflects the rise and decline of a state's political strength and changes of social customs. Music education fosters good governance and social stability. In an age of peace and stability with enlightened governance and harmony, its music and poetry are characterized by serenity and joyfulness. "Music of an age of good order" also refers to some eulogies in *The Book of Songs*.

引例 Citation：

◎凡音者，生人心者也。情动于中，故形于声。声成文，谓之音。是故治世之音安以乐，其政和。(《礼记·乐记》)
（大凡音乐都产生于人的内心。情感在心中激荡，所以表现为各种声音。声音组合成曲调，就叫做音乐。所以，太平时代的音乐祥和欢乐，这是因为政治宽和的缘故。）

All music is born in people's minds. As people's inner emotions surge, they turn into sound. When sound is formed into a pattern, music is created. The music of an age of good order is filled with peace and joyfulness thanks to the harmonious political atmosphere of the time. (*The Book of Rites*)

zhōnghé 中和

Balanced Harmony

人心所达到的中正、和谐的状态。人的喜、怒、哀、乐等情感的活动及其在言行上的表现符合礼的要求，不失偏颇进而达到一种和谐的状态，即是"中和"。治理者如果能够体认并达到"中和"的状态，以此治理天下，天地万物就会处于端正、恰当的位置，和谐、有序，就可以实现彼此间的共同繁荣与发展。

Balanced harmony is an ideal state of human mind. When people's emotions such as joy, anger, sorrow, and happiness are expressed in an unbiased way in keeping with the rites, a state of mind featuring balanced harmony is achieved. If a ruler can reach such a state of mind and exercise governance accordingly, everything in heaven and earth will be in its proper place, be orderly and in harmony with each other. This will deliver common prosperity and development for all.

引例 Citations：

◎喜怒哀乐之未发，谓之中；发而皆中（zhòng）节，谓之和。中也者，天下之大本也；和也者，天下之达道也。致中和，天地位焉，万物育焉。(《礼记·中庸》)

(喜怒哀乐还没有被事物感发时的状态，称作"中"；喜怒哀乐表现于言行而都能符合规范，称作"和"。"中"是天下的根本，"和"是天下最普遍的法则。治理者能够达到"中和"，天地就能处于正位，万物便可生长繁育了。)

When joy, anger, sorrow, and happiness are not yet expressed as a response to other things, they are in a state of balance. When they are expressed in words and deeds in accordance with the rites, harmony is achieved. Balance is the foundation under heaven, while harmony is the universal rule under heaven. If a ruler can achieve balanced harmony, both heaven and earth will be in their proper places, and all things will prosper and thrive. (*The Book of Rites*)

◎能以中和理天下者，其德大盛。能以中和养其身者，其寿极命。(董仲舒《春秋繁露·循天之道》)

(能够以"中和"治理天下的人，他的德政就会极大兴盛。能够以"中和"修养自身的人，他的寿命就会很长久。)

When one rules the world with balanced harmony, virtuous governance will flourish. When one achieves balanced harmony in self-cultivation, he will enjoy longevity. (Dong Zhongshu: *Luxuriant Gems of The Spring and Autumn Annals*)

zìshēng 自生

Spontaneous Generation

万物由自己生成。万物不由"天"或"无"创造产生，也不由其他有形的事物所产生。"自生"之说意在打破造物主的观念。对于万物"自生"的具体情形，人们有不同的理解。有人认为，"自生"的事物之间是相互关联、相互依赖的。但也有人主张，万物各自无联系地、孤立地、突然地"自生"。

Everything comes into being by itself; it is not created or generated by heaven, void, or tangible things. The expression "spontaneous generation" rejects the concept of a creator. People have different views about the concrete circumstances of the "spontaneous generation" of things. Some believe that things which are "spontaneously generated" are interrelated and dependent on one another, while some others assert that everything is "spontaneously generated" by itself abruptly, unconnected with others.

引例 Citations：

◎ 夫至无者无以能生，故始生者自生也。（裴頠（wéi）《崇有论》，见《晋书·裴秀传附子頠》）

（"无"不能创生事物，因此最初生成的事物一定是自生的。）

Void cannot create things, so the earliest things that came into being must have done so by themselves. (Pei Wei: *A Discussion of Respecting Tangible Things*)

◎ 无既无矣，则不能生有。有之未生，又不能为生。然则生生者谁哉？块然而自生耳。（郭象《庄子注》卷一）

（"无"已经是虚无的，自然不能产生有形的事物。有形的事物还未生成，也不能作为创生者。那么创生其他事物的是谁呢？万物都是独自生成的。）

Void means non-existence and naturally cannot generate tangible things. Before tangible things come into being, there cannot be any creator. Then what creates things? Obviously everything is spontaneously generated. (Guo Xiang: *Annotations on Zhuangzi*)

zìyóu 自由

Acting Freely / Freedom

本义是由自己做主，依从自己的想法、意志、愿望行事，不受外来限制和约束。在古代中国，儒道都向往内心与生命不受拘系的自由。近代以来，它用作 liberty 和 freedom 的译词。作为专有名词，其含义主要有二：其一，指法律所规定并保护的国民享有其意志、行为不受干涉的权利，如言论、集会、宗教信仰等方面的自由。其二，哲学上指人对必然性的认识和对客观世界的改造的自由。它是建立在对自然、社会规律深刻把握的基础上，以人的全面发展为目的的自由，被认为是构建美好社会的核心价值之一。

The term means acting on one's own free will without being subject to external restrictions. In ancient China, both Confucians and Daoists longed for freedom both of the mind and in their lives. In modern times, this term has become the Chinese word for "liberty" and "freedom." As a technical term, it has two meanings. One is citizens' statutory and law-protected rights not to be interfered in their will and actions, such as freedom of speech, freedom of assembly, and freedom of religious belief. The other, philosophically, refers to freedom of people's understanding of necessity and their transformation of the objective world. Based on a profound understanding of the principles governing the nature and society and aiming to ensure individuals to achieve well-rounded development, freedom is considered one of the core values conducive to a good society.

引例 Citation：

◎外物尽已外，闲游且自由。（齐己《匡山寓居栖公》）
（一切皆为身外之物，四方游历身心自由。）

Realizing that all things are all external, I wander at leisure and freely follow my own inclinations. (Qi Ji: In Memory of a Recluse During My Residence on Mount Lu)

zuòwàng 坐忘

Forget the Difference and Opposition Between Self and the Universe

　　道家指破除自我与事物之间分别与对立的一种方式。出自《庄子·大宗师》。书中借由孔子（前551—前479）与颜回（前521—前481）的对话阐述"坐忘"之义。庄子（前369？—前286）认为，人世中的各种名分、规范，造成了自我与事物之间的分别与对立，构成了对人的限制。人应该忘记这些名分、规范，进而忘记自己形体的存在与智力的运用，打破彼我之间的界限，从而摆脱外物的限制与影响，这便是"坐忘"。

The term refers to a Daoist way of breaking away from the difference and opposition between one's self and the universe. It comes from the book *Zhuangzi*, which elaborates its meaning in a dialogue between Confucius (551-479 BC) and Yan Hui (521-481 BC). In Zhuangzi's (369?-286 BC) view, status and etiquette norms in the human world caused divisions and antagonisms and hence created constraints on people. One should forget status and norms and furthermore forget one's own physical existence and intellect to cast off the differences between one's self and the universe and thus be free from the constraints and influence of external factors.

引例 Citation：

◎曰："回坐忘矣。"仲尼蹴（cù）然曰："何谓坐忘？"颜回曰："堕肢体，黜聪明，离形去知（zhì），同于大通，此谓坐忘。"（《庄子·大宗师》）
（颜回说："我坐忘了。"孔子惊奇地说："什么叫坐忘？"颜回说："不着意于自己的肢体，放弃自己的视听，超脱形体，摒除心智，与万物融通一体，这就是'坐忘'。")

Yan Hui said, "I forget." Startled, Confucius asked, "What do you mean by forgetting?" Yan Hui answered, "Pay no attention to my body and give up what I hear and see, leave the physical form, get rid of what occupies my mind, and become one with the universe. This is what I call forgetting the difference and opposition between myself and the universe." (*Zhuangzi*)

术语表 List of Concepts

英文	中文
Acting Freely / Freedom	自由
Baixi (All Performing Arts)	百戏
Balanced Harmony	中和
Be Totally Absorbed (in Reading and Learning)	涵泳
Benefit the People	惠民
Broad Love Extending to All	泛爱
Change Social Practices and Customs	移风易俗
Chinese Dragon	龙
Classical Prose Movement	古文运动
Clear the Mind of Enigmas	解蔽
Complete Man	成人
Conduct Oneself with a Sense of Shame	行己有耻
Conform Upwardly	尚同
Cross-checking and Verification	参验
Distinctiveness and Spontaneity	标举兴会
Do Not Do to Others What You Do Not Want Others to Do to You.	己所不欲，勿施于人
Do not Engage the Enemy If Victory Is Not Guaranteed.	不战在我
Dry Plainness	枯淡

英文	中文
Established Through Popular Usage / Accepted Through Common Practice	约定俗成
Exalt the Worthy	尚贤
Examine / Study	格
Extensive Love to Benefit All People	博爱
Fair / Just	公正
Filial Piety	孝
Food Is of Primary Importance to the People.	民以食为天
Forget the Difference and Opposition Between Self and the Universe	坐忘
Four Images	四象
Fraternal Duty	悌
Free Flow of One's Mind	畅神
Frontier Poetry	边塞诗
Gongdiao (Musical Modes)	宫调
Great Man	大丈夫
Grim and Desolate	荒寒
Handling Internal Affairs Takes Precedence over External Affairs.	治内裁外
Harmony Is Most Precious.	和为贵
Have Love for the People, and Cherish All Things	仁民爱物

英文	中文
He Who Obtains the Support of the People Will Rise; He Who Loses the Support of the People Will Come to Ruin.	得人者兴，失人者崩
Human Nature Is Evil.	性恶
Human Nature Is Good.	性善
Hypocrite	乡愿
Idyllic Poetry	田园诗
Ji (Omen)	几
Landscape Poetry	山水诗
Law / Dharma	法
Live in Peace and Work in Contentment	安居乐业
Lord of the People / Democracy	民主
Love the People	爱民
Love the People in Accordance with Rules of Moral Conduct	爱人以德
Metaphysical Poetry	玄言诗
Music of a Failing State	亡国之音
Music of an Age of Disorder	乱世之音
Music of an Age of Good Order	治世之音
Natural Rules and Orderliness	天经地义
Opportune Time, Geographic Advantage, and Unity of the People	天时地利人和
Perpetual Growth and Change	生生

英文	中文
Philosophical Substance Through Artistic Appeal	理趣
Poetry of the Prime Tang Dynasty	盛唐之音
Poetry on History	咏史诗
Proactive Versus Prudent	狂狷
Pure State of the Mind	心斋
Recluse Poetry	隐逸诗
Refreshing Words and Exquisite Expressions	清词丽句
Rejection of Fatalism	非命
Resentment and Sting	怨刺
Restrain Yourself and Follow Social Norms	克己复礼
Revere the Fundamental and Dismiss the Specific	崇本息末
Revere the Fundamental and Keep the Specific Unchanged	崇本举末
Rule Through Non-action	无为而治
Set Moral Examples, Perform Great Deeds, and Spread Noble Ideas	三不朽
Spontaneous Generation	自生
Stability Is the Key to Governance.	政贵有恒
Subtle Suggestion	含蓄
The Great Wall	长城
The *Haofang* School / The Bold and Unconstrained School	豪放派
The Jian'an Literary Style	建安风骨

英文	中文
The Only Motion Is Returning.	反者道之动
The People's Will Is the Foundation of the State.	民心惟本
The Style of *The Spring and Autumn Annals*	春秋笔法
The Taikang Literary Style	太康体
The *Wanyue* School / The Graceful and Restrained School	婉约派
The World Belongs to All.	天下为公
The Xikun Poetic Style	西昆体
The Yellow River	黄河
The Yongming Poetic Style	永明体
The Zhengshi Literary Style	正始体
Those Who Like to Go to War Will Perish; Those Who Forget War Will Be in Danger.	好战必亡，忘战必危
Those Who Rely on Virtue Will Thrive; Those Who Rely on Force Will Perish.	恃德者昌，恃力者亡
Transformation of Things	物化
Turning a Crude Poem or Essay into a Literary Gem	点铁成金
Two Modes	两仪
Use War to Stop War	以战止战
Vital Energy	精气
When Facing an Opportunity to Exercise Benevolence, Do Not Yield.	当仁不让

英文	中文
When the Granaries Are Full, the People Follow Appropriate Rules of Conduct.	仓廪实而知礼节
Will of the People	民心
Win Without Resorting to War	不战而胜
Xuanti Poetry / Poetry in Prince Zhaoming's Favorite Style	选体
Yuanheng Lizhen	元亨利贞
Yue (Music)	乐
Yuefu Poetry	汉乐府

中国历史年代简表 A Brief Chronology of Chinese History

夏 Xia Dynasty		2070-1600 BC
商 Shang Dynasty		1600-1046 BC
周 Zhou Dynasty		1046-256 BC
周 Zhou Dynasty	西周 Western Zhou Dynasty	1046-771 BC
	东周 Eastern Zhou Dynasty	770-256 BC
秦 Qin Dynasty		221-206 BC
汉 Han Dynasty		206 BC-AD 220
汉 Han Dynasty	西汉 Western Han Dynasty	206 BC-AD 25
	东汉 Eastern Han Dynasty	25-220
三国 Three Kingdoms		220-280
三国 Three Kingdoms	魏 Kingdom of Wei	220-265
	蜀 Kingdom of Shu	221-263
	吴 Kingdom of Wu	222-280
晋 Jin Dynasty		265-420
晋 Jin Dynasty	西晋 Western Jin Dynasty	265-317
	东晋 Eastern Jin Dynasty	317-420
南北朝 Southern and Northern Dynasties		420-589
南北朝 Southern and Northern Dynasties	南朝 Southern Dynasties	420-589
	南朝 Southern Dynasties — 宋 Song Dynasty	420-479
	齐 Qi Dynasty	479-502
	梁 Liang Dynasty	502-557
	陈 Chen Dynasty	557-589

南北朝 Southern and Northern Dynasties	北朝 Northern Dynasties	北朝 Northern Dynasties	386-581
		北魏 Northern Wei Dynasty	386-534
		东魏 Eastern Wei Dynasty	534-550
		北齐 Northern Qi Dynasty	550-577
		西魏 Western Wei Dynasty	535-556
		北周 Northern Zhou Dynasty	557-581
隋 Sui Dynasty			581-618
唐 Tang Dynasty			618-907
五代 Five Dynasties			907-960
五代 Five Dynasties		后梁 Later Liang Dynasty	907-923
		后唐 Later Tang Dynasty	923-936
		后晋 Later Jin Dynasty	936-947
		后汉 Later Han Dynasty	947-950
		后周 Later Zhou Dynasty	951-960
宋 Song Dynasty			960-1279
宋 Song Dynasty		北宋 Northern Song Dynasty	960-1127
		南宋 Southern Song Dynasty	1127-1279
辽 Liao Dynasty			907-1125
西夏 Western Xia Dynasty			1038-1227
金 Jin Dynasty			1115-1234
元 Yuan Dynasty			1206-1368
明 Ming Dynasty			1368-1644
清 Qing Dynasty			1616-1911
中华民国 Republic of China			1912-1949
中华人民共和国 People's Republic of China			Founded on October 1, 1949